Every Day with Jesus

MAR/APR 2019

The Wonder of the Cross

'Let us fix our eyes on Jesus... who for the joy set before him endured the cross, scorning its shame'
Hebrews 12:2

Selwyn Hughes
Revised and updated by Mick Brooks

MIX
Paper from
responsible sources
FSC® C015900

A word of introduction...

The cross, despite being an overtly Christian symbol, is pretty much everywhere: in homes, in the movies, works of art, music videos and it's worn as tattoos, earrings and necklaces. It's even on several nations' flags. What wouldn't the big brand names give to own a symbol that countless millions of people wear and catch sight of almost daily!

Though a very simple shape, the cross is arguably one of the most powerful symbols in the world, but its impact and implications are rarely celebrated or even acknowledged. In many ways it's almost too familiar – so familiar that we often don't even see its influence and placing in modern society. The cross on which Jesus was executed 2,000 years ago has been the symbol used by the first Christians from very early on. Initially they were afraid to make a public display because of fear of persecution. However, when Emperor Constantine converted to Christianity in the fourth century, crucifixion was abolished as a punishment, and the cross became the symbol for Christianity.

The cross was originally a symbol of great pain and suffering, but Jesus turned what was meant for humiliation and defeat on its head. The cross is now, and will always be, seen as a symbol of redemption and salvation.

As we focus again this Easter on the wonder of the cross, my prayer is that we would be brought to our knees by the unrivalled love it represents.

Mick

Mick Brooks, Consulting Editor

Free small group resource to accompany this issue can be found at **www.cwr.org.uk/extra**

f The *EDWJ* Facebook community is growing!
To join the conversation visit **www.facebook.com/edwjpage**

A new application

'May I never boast except in the cross of our Lord Jesus Christ' (v14)

In these meditations, which include Easter, I invite you to reconsider the wonder of the cross. Although you may have thought about the cross many times over the years, today you will see and understand it differently from every previous occasion. This is because although the power and meaning of the cross never change, you do. You are not the same person today that you were yesterday. A famous philosopher said: 'If you were to step into a river, step out and step back in again, it would not be the same river, for the river you stepped into a few moments before has flowed on. Nothing is the same – everything changes.'

As far as this world is concerned, the philosopher has a point – everything changes. Because of the changes that have taken place in your life in the past months or years, even in the past 24 hours, you too have changed and will therefore approach the cross as a different person. Life has brought new things – perhaps a deep personal need, a family crisis, a bereavement, a financial loss, a betrayal by a friend – and because of this your need to embrace the cross as the meeting place between yourself and God is more real than ever. Maybe you're more personally vulnerable and you're less self-reliant. Maybe through life circumstances you're more spiritually apprehensive.

I repeat: although the cross and the power that flows from it have not changed, you have changed. By God's grace, the significance of things heard in the past will become fresher and newer, and though taking a fresh look at the cross may not result in a new revelation, it could well result in a new application.

FURTHER STUDY

Psa. 33:4–11, 18–22;
1 Cor. 15:1–11

1. How does the psalmist celebrate God's changeless and undying love?

2. What does Paul regard as being 'of first importance'?

My Father and my God, as I prepare to sit once again at the foot of the cross, please grant that the changes in me will make me more open to Your changeless and undying love. In Jesus' name I pray. Amen.

'We hear the way we are'

FOR READING & MEDITATION – PSALM 119:17–24

'Open my eyes that I may see wonderful things in your law.' (v18)

As we prepare to focus again on the cross, I would like to emphasise what I said yesterday: namely that although the meaning and power of the cross never change, we do. Dr Bruce Theilman expressed it like this: 'We hear and see things not just the way they are said or shown, but the way we are.' What he meant, I think, is this: we interpret the things we see and hear in a way that is very personal to us. For instance, two people listening to the same talk or sermon will understand what is said in different ways.

FURTHER STUDY

Matt. 16:21–26;
Acts 3:11–16;
1 Pet. 2:4–8

1. What changed Peter's view of the cross?

2. Contrast those who accept with those who reject the living stone.

Something that has intrigued me since I began writing *Every Day with Jesus* is that when I received a number of letters commenting on what I had written, I found that many people had actually interpreted the point entirely differently. In the early days as I looked back over what I had written, I would think, *But I didn't say what that person seems to have understood.* Bruce Theilman is right; we hear and see things not just the way they are said or written but the way we are.

Is it any wonder that the Bible holds such fascination for Christians who meditate on it day by day? A text we may have read yesterday comes alive to us today in a completely new way, not because its meaning has changed – real truth never changes – but because in our new personal situation we discover a new way of applying and engaging with it. It is the same with the cross. The meaning of the cross never changes, but in the coming weeks it may well be that you understand it more fully, hear the truth about it with greater insight and come to see its significance in a way that you have never seen it before.

Gracious heavenly Father, grant that it may be so. Let the old, old story of Jesus and the cross come home to me with a freshness that I have never known before. In Jesus' name I pray. Amen.

No gospel without a cross

FOR READING & MEDITATION – GALATIANS 3:1–14

'Before your very eyes Jesus Christ was clearly portrayed as crucified.' (v1)

The universally recognised symbol of Christianity is a cross. This is significant, as there are several other symbols the Church could have chosen as the sign of the Christian faith. I can think of at least seven possibilities: the manger in which He was laid as a baby; the carpenter's bench at which He worked; the dove, which was the form taken by the Holy Spirit when He descended on Jesus at His baptism; the boat from which He taught the people in Galilee; the basin He used when He washed the disciples' feet; the stone that was rolled away from the tomb in which His dead body was resurrected; or the heavenly throne from which He came and to which He returned at His ascension. Any of these seven symbols could have been chosen by the Church to symbolise the Christian faith, but instead the selected symbol is a cross. Why is this?

The cross was chosen because the early Christians wished to make known that central to the ministry of Jesus was not His birth, His teaching, His miracles, or even His resurrection but His death and crucifixion. Without that we could not have been reconciled to God. There is no gospel without the cross. To preach the gospel is to portray Jesus not primarily as a baby in a cradle, a worker of miracles, a preacher and teacher of distinction, but as the crucified Saviour. It is this that gives the gospel its power. As the apostle Paul tells us in our text for today, only when Christ is 'clearly portrayed as crucified' is the gospel taught. The good news of the gospel is that through Jesus' atoning death and victorious resurrection, we have been given new life.

FURTHER STUDY

Acts 5:27–32;
Rom. 6:1–10

1. How did Peter clearly portray Christ as crucified?

2. What connection does Paul make between Christ's death and baptism?

Blessed Saviour, how can I ever sufficiently thank You for going down into death so that I might have everlasting life? All honour and glory be to Your name for ever. Amen.

'Blood on our hands'

FOR READING & MEDITATION – ACTS 4:23–31

'Herod and Pontius Pilate met together with the Gentiles and the people of Israel... to conspire against... Jesus' (v27)

The presentation of Mel Gibson's film *The Passion of the Christ*, first shown some years ago, caused many to believe that it would let loose an avalanche of distrust towards the Jews for their seeming complicity in the trial and death of Jesus. Such, however, has not been the case. Those who use Christ's crucifixion as a justification for anti-Semitism dishonour the name of Jesus. We cannot pretend that the Jews who acted to bring about the death of Jesus were entirely innocent, but we must see that others were implicated in it too.

FURTHER STUDY

Acts 2:36–41; 3:17–26

1. How does Peter answer the people's question on the Day of Pentecost?

2. In what way does Peter link Jesus' death with our repentance?

In the passage before us today, the writer Luke tells us that Herod and Pontius Pilate and other Gentiles conspired against Jesus. So Gentiles had a part in it as well as Jews. The way to avoid anti-Semitic prejudice in connection with the crucifixion of Jesus is to realise that, had we been living at the time, we would have done the very same thing. Do you struggle with that idea? Then consider this: whenever you have pursued your own interests instead of God's, whenever you have chosen to be envious or put your own ambitions before God's will for your life then you have, in effect, crucified the Son of God afresh.

The old spiritual song asks the question, 'Were you there when they crucified my Lord?' We may not have been there as spectators but we were certainly there as participants. The sins that nailed Jesus to the cross are in us as well. There is blood on our hands also. John Stott, writing on this, says: 'Before we can begin to see the cross as something done for us (leading us to faith and worship) we have to see it as something done by us (leading us to repentance).'

Lord Jesus Christ, forgive us when we fail to see that not only those who crucified You are responsible for Your death; the guilt is on our hands too. Thank You, however, for Your free and wonderful forgiveness. In Jesus' name. Amen.

CWR Ministry Events

PLEASE PRAY FOR THE TEAM

DATE	EVENT	PLACE	PRESENTER(S)
8 Mar	Waverley Abbey College Open Day	Waverley Abbey House	WAC team
8–10 Mar	Bible Discovery Weekend	WAH	Philip Greenslade
9 Mar	Understanding Yourself, Understanding Others	WAH	Rosalyn and Steve Derges
13 Mar	How to Answer Your Friends' Questions About Faith	WAH	Andy Peck
15–17 Mar	Inspiring Women Spring Weekend: Free to Be Me	WAH	Nicki Copeland and Rosie Morgan
16 Mar	Insight into Self-Acceptance	WAH	Chris Ledger
23 Mar	Boundaries	WAH	Kara Lawman and team
27 Mar	Small Group Essentials	WAH	Andy Peck
3 Apr	Inspiring Women Spring Day: Encounters That Change Us	WAH	Jen Flanagan
8–12 Apr	Introduction to Biblical Care and Counselling	WAH	Louise Dyer, Rob Jackson and team
17 Apr	Passover Supper	WAH	Elizabeth Hodkinson
25 Apr	Pastoral Care from Scratch	WAH	Andy Peck
26 Apr	Pastoring on the Fringe	WAH	Andy Peck

Please pray for our students and tutors on our ongoing courses in Counselling and Spiritual Formation at Waverley Abbey College (taking place at Waverley Abbey House).

We would also appreciate prayer for our ongoing ministry in Singapore and Cambodia, as well as the many regional events that will be happening around the UK this year.

For further information and a full list of CWR's courses, seminars and events, call **(+44) 01252 784719** or visit **cwr.org.uk/courses**

You can also download our free Prayer Track, which includes daily prayers, from **cwr.org.uk/prayertrack**

Reconciled to God

FOR READING & MEDITATION – ROMANS 5:1–11

'we also rejoice in God through our Lord Jesus Christ, through whom we have now received reconciliation.' (v11)

It is fashionable for people to wear a cross as a piece of jewellery even though they do not appear to have any interest or understanding of what the cross stands for. One young woman was overheard in a jeweller's shop asking if she could have a cross 'with a little man on it'. It's sad that many who choose a cross to wear have no real understanding of its life-changing implications. So what does the cross really signify? We shall explore this in more depth, but as a starting point for our journey, consider this thought: the cross made reconciliation possible between sinful humanity and a holy God.

FURTHER STUDY

Eph. 2:13–22;
Heb. 4:14–16

1. Reflect on what access to God really means.

2. Why is it we can approach the throne of grace with confidence?

The word 'reconciliation' in today's text signifies a restoration to favour or an exchange on the behalf of one party, induced by an action on the part of another. As Paul highlights in verse 10, our sin actually made us God's enemies, but Christ's death has made it possible for us to have a relationship with Him. In the Authorised Version today's text reads, 'we also joy in God through our Lord Jesus Christ, by whom we have now received the atonement'. Though this is not the most accurate translation, the word 'atonement' shows us what God has done for us in making us at one with Himself. In *The Cross of Christ*, John Stott says: 'Reconciliation is the meaning of the atonement. It alludes to the event through which God and human beings, previously alienated from one another, are made "at one" again.'

How glorious to realise that God, from whom we were once estranged by reason of our sin, has reconciled us to Himself through the death of His Son. God hand in hand with those who were once His enemies – can anything be more wonderful?

Loving heavenly Father, I see that through the Saviour's death on the cross, a door has been opened for me to come into Your presence. I run through that door with open arms and into Your loving embrace. Amen.

The coining of a word

FOR READING & MEDITATION – ROMANS 3:21–31

'God presented him as a sacrifice of atonement, through faith in his blood.' (v25)

The word 'atonement', which we mentioned yesterday, has a fascinating history. In the sixteenth century, when William Tyndale was translating the New Testament and parts of the Old Testament into English so that ordinary people could read the Bible, he encountered a number of difficulties. One of those was that the language of his day was inadequate to express the full meaning of the Greek and Hebrew from which he was translating.

Particularly baffling was the problem of finding a word that would convey the beauty and wonder of the term Paul used in Greek to describe the reconciling and redeeming work of the Lord Jesus Christ. Having failed to discover an adequate expression, Tyndale was reduced to the expedient of inventing one. Joining two words together – 'at' and 'onement' – he coined a word which has been used by theologians since that time to define the doctrine of Christ's substitutionary death on the cross.

However, many modern Christian writers avoid using this word as it has been adopted by those interested in spirituality, who bend its meaning out of recognition. Quite correctly, they say the word 'atonement' means 'at-one-ment', but they interpret this as 'oneness with the One' – a mystical idea that identifies God with the universe and fails to distinguish the creation from its Creator. We should not for that reason be shy of using the word; rather, we should reclaim it and reinstate it by showing that Jesus' atoning death made it possible for a holy God to offer us forgiveness for our sin and for God and humankind to live together in perfect harmony and peace.

FURTHER STUDY

2 Chron. 29:20–24;
Prov. 16:6;
1 John 1:8–2:2

1. How did Old Testament sacrifices foreshadow the sacrifice of Jesus?

2. List the benefits that come to us through Jesus' atoning death.

Father, as I dwell on Christ's atonement, please help me to see it not merely as a rule of doctrine but as a release of life. Move the truth from my head to my heart, I pray. In Jesus' name. Amen.

Jesus is the Atonement

FOR READING & MEDITATION – HEBREWS 2:5–18

'he had to be made like his brothers in every way, in order that he might become a merciful and faithful high priest' (v17)

There is one aspect of the atonement that is sometimes overlooked when we consider this wonderful truth, and it is this: it is important to say that we should not become so preoccupied with the cross that we miss the Person who died upon it.

Dr Edwards of Bala, a Welsh theologian, set out to write a book on the subject of Jesus' atoning death. After writing a few pages, there burst upon his heart such a revelation of the Person of Christ that, jumping up from his desk, he ran out into the street shouting excitedly, 'Jesus is the Atonement! Jesus is the Atonement!' Returning to his study, he wrote these inspiring words: 'This is the Atonement – not the sufferings and not the death but the Person of the Son of God in the sufferings and the death. It is not that He made the Atonement, or paid the Atonement. The Bible goes far beyond that. He is the Atonement – not He Himself without the act, but He Himself in the act.'

Although we will not focus specifically on the incarnation in these meditations (as our thoughts are focused mainly on the cross), I feel that mention must be made of it before we continue. Jesus had to share in our humanity before He could give Himself to us in redemption. Those who do not trust in the virgin birth are unlikely to fully grasp the meaning of the cross, as the one depends on the other. If Jesus had not joined Himself to us in the incarnation, He would not have been able to join us to God through His redemption. 'A Saviour who is not quite God,' said one person, 'is like a bridge broken at one end.' It is not a criminal's death on a cross that saves but the Son of God who hung upon it.

FURTHER STUDY

Matt. 1:20–25;
Luke 1:67–75;
2:8–14

1. What does the name 'Jesus' signify?

2. How were redemption and salvation announced at Jesus' birth?

God my Father, help me never to forget that however much I study the doctrine of the atonement, it is not the doctrine that saves but the Person – the Person of Your Son. In Him I rest my faith for all eternity. Amen.

A new horizon

FOR READING & MEDITATION – ROMANS 1:1–7

*'his Son... was declared with power to be the Son of God, by his
resurrection from the dead: Jesus Christ our Lord.' (vv3–4)*

Before we move on, let's remember that the New
Testament always joins together the atonement and Jesus'
resurrection. The text before us today tells us that Christ was
'declared with power to be the Son of God'. What does to be
'declared with power' mean? The word translated 'declared'
comes from the Greek word *horizo* – the word from which we
get our English word 'horizon'. The resurrection of Jesus has
given the world a completely new horizon.

One minister explained it like this: 'Imagine a television
news studio before the high-powered lights are
switched on. The newsreader who sits there occupies
just a few cubic feet of space. If someone was able to
see him from a mile away he would look very small
indeed. And if he shouted with his loudest voice he
would not be heard. But when the lights are switched
on and the cameras begin to roll – what a difference.
He can now be seen and heard by millions.'

Since the resurrection, Jesus, who from His birth to
His death had occupied just a few cubic feet of space
and could only be in one place at a time, is now able
to fulfil His promise that 'where two or three come
together in my name, there am I with them' (Matt. 18:20). He
was with me as these notes were written and He is with you as
you read them today. On that glorious resurrection morning,
Jesus pushed back all horizons, and through His rising from
the dead has opened up for us not just new perspectives here
on earth but also the unending vistas of eternity. There is a
song that says, 'I can see clearly now the rains have gone.' My
heart sings, 'I can see clearly now that Christ has risen.' How
about you?

**FURTHER
STUDY**

1 Cor. 15:1–8;
2 Tim. 1:8–14

1. What did Paul
say is of first
importance?

2. What has
Jesus brought
to light through
the gospel?

**Father, I am so thankful that Your Son's resurrection has opened up
for me many new horizons. I see the past, present and future in a
new light. Everything is full of joyous hope. I am so grateful. Amen.**

Salvation has to be received

FOR READING & MEDITATION – JOHN 1:1–18

'Yet to all who received him, to those who believed in his name,
he gave the right to become children of God' (v12)

We continue on our journey of rediscovery of the wondrous cross and the atonement. A few days ago we touched on how some modern Christian writers avoid using the word 'atonement' because of a mystical spirituality emphasis, but that is no reason, we said, to avoid it. Instead, the word needs to be reclaimed and understood in its biblical context. You may recollect also that I concluded by focusing on the truth that Christ's atoning death brought humankind into a new relationship with a holy God and made it possible for God and the people He has created to live together in perfect harmony and peace.

FURTHER STUDY

Acts 16:25–34;
1 John 4:1–6;
5:1–5

1. How did the Philippian jailer find salvation?

2. How does John describe those who are born of God?

I use the word 'possible', as the reconciliation between us and God is realised only when we acknowledge what He has done for us and respond by surrendering our lives to Jesus. Multitudes of people hold the dangerous idea that Christ's atoning death on the cross means the debt of human sin has been paid and that everyone is automatically forgiven. Through the cross, God reaches out to humanity, but it is only as they respond to Him in willing submission that they can experience the benefits of His Son's atonement. Forgiveness has to be received before it can take effect in our lives.

At many a funeral I have heard compassionate church leaders attempt to comfort the bereaved by saying that on the cross Jesus paid the debt for our sins, which means that now everyone is entitled to go to heaven when they die – whether they believed or not. That is what the apostle Paul would call 'another gospel'. Heaven, as today's text clearly implies, is open 'to all who received him, to those who believed in his name'.

Father, forgive us, as Your Church, that so often in the interests of other people's comfort we preach another gospel. Help us see that to give false comfort is to endanger people to a lost eternity. In Jesus' name. Amen.

The wonder of brokenness

At the heart of CWR's ministry is the desire to connect people, whatever their struggles and triumphs, with the truths of the Bible in a way that will transform lives and relationships. The parents of a son with a life-limiting illness and complex needs, Rachel and Tim Wright have written a new devotional book to help people face difficulties with honesty, vulnerability, and humour. Here they are in their own words...

'When our son was born with severe and complex brain damage, our hearts and dreams lay broken. We were shattered. Through this 40-window devotional, we want to share how brokenness became our invitation to wholehearted living.

The life of Jesus shows us the heart and character of God. He entered humanity by sitting in the mess with us. He was laid in a manger, walked the dusty streets, died on a cross and rose again with the scars of suffering etched on His hands. Those at the time were shocked and baffled by this humble, broken demonstration of God. So we invite you to join us in discovering how God has, and always will, give us the greatest view through the broken windows of our lives.'

Shattered: God's view through life's broken windows by Rachel and Tim Wright is available March 2019. For prices and to purchase, visit **cwr.org.uk/shop** or your local Christian bookshop.

Open the door

FOR READING & MEDITATION – JOHN 5:16–30

'whoever hears my word and believes him who sent me has eternal life and will not be condemned' (v24)

Today we continue meditating on the truth that in order to be sure we go to heaven when we die, we must apply the work that Jesus did on the cross by personally accepting Him as Saviour and Lord. For those who fail to do this and ignore His sacrifice, the situation is as if the atonement had never taken place.

Evangelists emphasise that in the United Kingdom, the laws designed to protect the rights of citizens mean that not even the Queen herself dare enter uninvited into the dwelling of the humblest subject. Imagine the Queen of England waiting on your doorstep to be invited in! But there is something more amazing still: the Lord Jesus Christ, Creator of the universe, will not step over the threshold of your heart unless invited.

FURTHER STUDY

1 Pet. 1:1–6;
Rev. 3:19–22

1. For what does Peter say we can praise God?

2. What does Jesus promise to those who open the door?

How does a person become a child of God? Well, how does anyone become a child at all? Is it not by birth? This was the very point in the passage we looked at yesterday: 'children born not of natural descent, nor of human decision or a husband's will, but born of God' (John 1:13). Notice the three things about spiritual birth that John mentions: 'not of natural descent, nor of human decision or a husband's will'. Salvation is not the result of human endeavour but human surrender. Jesus comes in only when He is invited. And how do we invite Him into our life? I cannot do better than to highlight the wonderfully simple words of Dr Alexander Maclaren: 'When I open my eyes the light comes in, when I open my lungs the air comes in, when I open my heart to Christ, then Christ comes in.' If you have not already done so, will you not open the door of your heart and let Him in? Remember, the handle is on your side.

Lord Jesus Christ, my heart is open to You at this moment. Come in and save me from my sins. Give me the gift of eternal life and make me a true child of God this very day I pray. Amen.

Children have to be born

FOR READING & MEDITATION – ROMANS 8:9–17

'those who are led by the Spirit of God are sons of God.' (v14)

In order to gather up any hesitant readers who may not as yet have made a decision to receive Jesus, let's spend another day exploring this most important matter of salvation.

Millions have the idea that everyone born into the human family is a child of God. Often people say: 'Doesn't the universal Fatherhood of God mean that we all belong to Him and one day will find ourselves at home with Him in heaven?' There is, however, a great difference between being a child of creation and a child of redemption. Beyond all question, Jesus taught that God is the Father of all men and women in the sense that He is their Creator. Yet He did not hesitate to declare that certain Jews belonged to their father the devil (John 8:44). Similarly the apostle Paul, in his address to the Athenians, quoted approvingly one of their poets to the effect that all men and women are God's offspring, but he would never have dreamt of saying to them, as he actually did to his converts, 'You are children of God' (Gal. 3:26).

I read once of a man called 'Stewart', who believed that he was descended from the royal house of Scotland – the Stewarts (or Stuarts as the name is more commonly spelt). Once he started to research his family tree, however, he learnt that one of his ancestors was named 'Stywart' and had been a pig-keeper in Norfolk! Many go through life making a similar mistake – thinking they are children of God when in fact they are not His children at all. The text we looked at two days ago said we 'become' children of God. Become – notice that. It is a word of vital significance. Today God invites you to become a child of God by faith in His name.

FURTHER STUDY

Matt. 11:25–30;
Acts 16:11–15;
19:1–7;
Titus 3:3–7

1. Who is it that knows the Father?

2. How does Paul say God saves us?

Heavenly Father, nothing in this world can be more important than my soul's salvation. Help me not to procrastinate and therefore miss heaven's eternal peace with You. In Jesus' name. Amen.

Do I need to understand it?

FOR READING & MEDITATION – 1 CORINTHIANS 1:18–31

'For the message of the cross is foolishness to those who are perishing, but to us… it is the power of God.' (v18)

As we continue our meditations on the wondrous cross, let's explore some of the common questions that come into people's minds as they consider this momentous event in history. It is not surprising that the cross, which really is the greatest mystery in the universe, raises questions that the human mind seeks to answer.

One of the questions often asked about Christ's death on the cross takes this form: is it necessary to understand the various theories concerning the cross in order to be saved by it? No. The cross embraces everyone, from the most literate to the uneducated, providing they reach out in simple faith and appropriate the power that lies within it. Our inability to comprehend how the death of Christ atones for sin makes no difference to its power to save, providing, as I said, we know how to reach out in simple faith.

At one time I lived under the flight path of the British Airways' Concorde – now taken out of service. Every day it used to roar over my home as it flew to the USA, and for a minute or two it was impossible to concentrate. I would think to myself, 'I doubt if even a dozen people on board know anything about aerodynamics and understand how the aircraft can fly across the Atlantic faster than the speed of sound.' They did not know and they did not care. Very soon they would land in the United States, put their watches back several hours, and go about their business. Concorde provided an ultra fast flight though only a few would have understood the technicalities of it. So it is with the cross. It can provide for those who do not understand, so long as they trust themselves to it.

FURTHER STUDY

Acts 8:26–38; 10:39–48

1. How did the Ethiopian respond to the mystery of the cross?

2. How did Cornelius respond to the gospel?

God my Father, what a relief it is that although I am unable to fathom all the mystery of the cross, I can still take hold of its saving power. Even if the light of my understanding is small there is sunlight in my heart. Amen.

It was for me

FOR READING & MEDITATION – 1 CORINTHIANS 15:20–28

'For as in Adam all die, so in Christ all will be made alive.' (v22)

Another question often raised by people regarding the cross is this: how can the cross save me now when the crucifixion took place close on 2,000 years before I was born? Well, the fact that something was done before you were born does not render it useless as you will discover if, in a time of desperate need, you find yourself benefiting from it.

Have you ever required an anaesthetic because you needed an operation? As the doctor explained just what would happen, weren't you glad that some time in the past anaesthetic was discovered? Just imagine what a major operation would be like without anaesthetic! I once read the account of an operation done some centuries ago before the discovery of anaesthetic. My stomach turned as I read the description of the surgeon performing an amputation. You can see, I am sure, that although anaesthetic was discovered before you were born, you can benefit from it now. It would be pointless to argue and say, 'No, anaesthetic wasn't discovered for me, it was for someone else.'

Though Sir James Simpson could not have foreseen our existence in the world when he discovered chloroform as an anaesthetic, we now can say in a sense, 'It was for me.' God, however, did foresee us – and so each of us can truly claim of our Lord's death on the cross, 'It was for me'! His death avails for us. Along with the hymnist we can say:

> *It was for me, yes, all for me,*
> *The Saviour died on Calvary.*
> *For me!*

FURTHER STUDY

Rom. 5:15–21;
15:5–13

1. Why might we give thanks for the obedience of one man?

2. Use Paul's prayers as a basis for your own doxology.

Lord Jesus Christ, my Saviour and Redeemer, I look at the cross and say with conviction, 'It was for me, yes, all for me.' Thank You for helping me realise that the gift of salvation was for me. Amen.

'I did that'

FOR READING & MEDITATION – 1 TIMOTHY 1:12–20

'The grace of our Lord was poured out on me abundantly, along with the faith and love that are in Christ Jesus.' (v14)

Another question people sometimes raise when they think about the cross is this: how can my sins be atoned for by Jesus when He actually died centuries before I committed any? Well, Jesus Christ died not only for our sins but because of our sins. Let us recall the old hymn we referred to earlier: 'Were you there when they crucified my Lord?' Some versions of this song have a concluding verse that says, 'I was there when they crucified my Lord.'

But in what sense can it be said that you and I were there at the cross when Jesus died? It means that we were represented there – represented by the people who were involved in the death of Jesus. You might say, 'Wasn't Jesus put to death by a few evil-inspired godless men? I would never plot the death of anyone. How can I have been represented at the cross?' Well, difficult though it may be for some to understand, all sin breaks God's original design, which includes our attitudes as well as actions, such as prejudice, self-centredness and indifference. All of these were in evidence at the cross. Can you honestly stand up and say that you have never been prejudiced, selfish or indifferent? But even if you answer, 'No, I have never committed these sins,' always remember that deep within the heart of each of us, there is a stubborn commitment to independence that resists accepting Jesus' rule and lordship over our lives – and so all of us are sinners.

No, you may not have been at the cross, but you were certainly represented there. Whenever you think about the wondrous cross, pause and ask God to help you understand and appreciate its impact on your life – here and in eternity.

FURTHER STUDY

Psa. 103:1–12;
Eph. 5:1–2,8–10

1. What are the benefits that flow from the cross?

2. What effect should the sacrifice of Jesus have on us?

Jesus, I'm beginning to understand that I was represented at Calvary, just as if my own hands had hammered in the nails. But now I am forgiven, redeemed, restored and reconciled. All glory be to Your wonderful and precious name. Amen.

It had to be

FOR READING & MEDITATION – LUKE 24:13–35

'Did not the Christ have to suffer these things and then enter his glory?' (v26)

We think now about yet another question, which is often asked by people when they consider the cross: Couldn't God find a way to forgive without the need for Jesus to die on the cross? After all, God is able to do anything, isn't He? This is a challenging question of taxing theology, which I believe we will never truly understand this side of eternity. However, the simple answer to the question is this: God could not find a way to forgive without the cross. There was no way that sin could be forgiven except by a divine atonement.

As to the second part of the question: 'After all, God is able to do anything, isn't He?' Indeed, Jesus Himself said, 'with God all things are possible'. To understand this, we really need to consider the other side of God's nature, as Scripture also tells us, 'it is impossible for God to lie' (Heb. 6:18). God cannot deny His own loving nature – be vindictive, evil or unkind. As Paul says in 2 Timothy 2:13, 'He cannot disown himself.' So whenever we say, 'God can do anything,' our statement must be understood in the light of the whole of God's nature.

God could not forgive sin without the cross because the consequence of sin is death – both spiritual and physical. Sin carries death in its nature more lethally than the bite of a black mamba. The human race is so infected with the disease of sin that it had to be exposed at Calvary and its devastating consequences destroyed by the sacrificial death of the Son of God. What we know of the character and nature of God is this: if the cross was unnecessary then God would not have sent His Son to die in the place of us.

FURTHER STUDY

Rom. 6:15–23;
Heb. 9:23–28

1. For what ought we to give thanks, according to Paul?

2. How did Jesus do away with sin?

Dear Lord, I am amazed as I consider the awe-inspiring paradox of the cross. Although the crucifixion was the greatest crime the world has ever known, it was also the greatest revelation of Your love. Thank You Lord Jesus. Amen.

God's motive in giving Christ

FOR READING & MEDITATION – EPHESIANS 2:1–10

'But because of his great love for us, God, who is rich in mercy, made us alive with Christ' (vv4–5)

N ow that we have reflected on some of the more common questions that arise in people's minds when they contemplate the cross, I would like to spend a few days considering the motive in God's heart in allowing His Son to leave heaven's glory and give His life for us on a Roman gibbet. Was the motive justice? Or righteousness? Or honour? Or was it something else?

Down the centuries, since the death of Christ, the Christian Church has devised and propounded many theories concerning why God gave His Son to die on the cross. One theory says the cross was motivated by the righteousness of God. The moral order, which had been upset by sin, needed to be re-established, and therefore Christ died so that the balance of the universe in terms of righteousness should be restored. God was obliged to show that it is impossible for sin to get the better of Him. He must not only be right, but be seen to be right – hence the cross. Yet another theory claims that God's motive was to strike a commercial bargain with the devil – a payment to him so that men and women could be released from his grip.

FURTHER STUDY

2 Thess. 2:13–17; 3:5; 1 John 3:16–24

1. How do we discover what love is?

2. How did Paul express God's heartbeat of love?

Another view of the cross, which is certainly rooted in Scripture, is that of divine justice. God, because of His nature, must punish sin, and thus the cross became the lightning conductor through which God's anger towards sin could be expressed. But God's chief motive in sending His Son was love (see 1 John 4:10). Charles Wesley got it right when he wrote:

Love led Him to die, and on this we rely,
He hath loved, He hath loved us. We cannot tell why.

Father, thank You for allowing me to feel the beat of Your heart – Your heart which beats with the energy of everlasting love. I am truly grateful. Amen.

The greatest thing about God

FOR READING & MEDITATION – 1 JOHN 4:1–12

'This is love: not that we loved God, but that he loved us and sent his Son as an atoning sacrifice for our sins.' (v10)

Yesterday we said that God's overriding motive in sending His Son to die on a cross was not righteousness, justice or honour, but love. All God's attributes were involved, of course, but the main motive for our salvation came from His unconditional and everlasting love. God's holiness is what He stands for; God's righteousness is what He does; God's justice is what He demands; God's love is who and what He is. It is love that holds and measures all God's attributes. Justice and holiness would send us away from God. Love, however, caused God to give His Son as a sacrifice – which satisfies the demands of justice and holiness, enabling us, through faith and repentance, to approach Him and be as familiar with Him as a child with a loving earthly father.

FURTHER STUDY

Psa. 117:1–2; 118:1–4, 28–29; John 17:20–26

1. What does the psalmist say we should praise God and give thanks for?

2. How does Jesus Himself acknowledge God's love?

The Christian Church is frequently in danger of presenting the gospel in an unbalanced way and going to extremes. For example, it may over-emphasise God's justice and His holiness and be weak on emphasising His love or vice versa. Although we should be careful not to ignore God's standards and the other attributes of His Person, I feel we must make it plain that the main motivation behind the message of redemption is that God loves us.

In my youth I heard many of the Welsh preachers who visited my church talk about God's justice, righteousness and wrath. I was frightened and overawed by those sermons – but I still resisted the call to salvation. One night I heard a preacher say that while God was angry at my sin, He loved me. It won my heart. That was now decades ago – and I never got over it!

Lord God, Your words and my needs fit each other. My greatest need is to be loved – and what do I find? The greatest thing about You is love. I will never cease to praise You. Amen.

He is crazy about us

FOR READING & MEDITATION – JOHN 3:1–16

'whoever believes in him shall not perish but have eternal life.' (v16)

No one should think that in emphasising God's love I am belittling the different theories that people hold concerning the cross. Yes, God's righteousness, holiness and honour were involved, but the point I am making is that the chief motivation was His great and unending love. We must not ignore or deny the truth of God's justice, His enmity towards sin, and all the other truths contained in Scripture, but the main thrust of the gospel message is always, as today's text puts it, that 'God so loved the world that he gave his one and only Son'. As Robert Walmsley wrote in his hymn *Wonderful Love*:

FURTHER STUDY

Psa. 139:1–10;
John 13:1–5,
12–17, 34–35

1. How well did God know the psalmist?

2. What is to be the measure and extent of our love?

> *Wonderful love*
> *dwells in the heart*
> *of the Father above.*

For my entire ministry I have looked at this verse and been overwhelmed by it. I have preached on it hundreds of times, but I still feel that to try and expound it is to spoil it – like picking a rose to emphasise its beauty.

Our reading today, from John's Gospel, has been described as 'the high watermark of revelation' or 'the gospel in a nutshell'. Nothing we can ever know about God is greater than this. The text sets it out in words that are precise and crystal clear. There can be no possible mistake – God really does love us. To put it in modern parlance, He is crazy about us. Whoever else might not be crazy about you, keep this thought always in your mind – God is.

Father God, how thankful I am that You don't just like me but that You are crazy about me. You think about me continuously. I am never out of Your thoughts. May my love come closer and closer to Yours, I pray. Amen.

Love unfailing

FOR READING & MEDITATION – PSALM 48:1–14

'Within your temple, O God, we meditate on your unfailing love.' (v9)

The text we looked at yesterday – John 3:16 – is without doubt the clearest declaration to be found anywhere in Scripture of God's motive in sending His Son to the cross.

The Old Testament clearly portrays the fact that God is a loving God, but as A.C. Dixon, one-time minister of the Metropolitan Tabernacle in London, pointed out, the references to God's love are somewhat overshadowed by the hundreds of texts that depict Him as full of holy wrath. He tells how one day he decided to preach a series of sermons on the love of God. His first thought was to go through the Bible book by book and preach on the various passages on God's love, but to his surprise he did not find as many as he expected. There are numerous verses in the Old Testament, of course, that depict God as being loving, as we see from the psalm we have read today, but Dixon remarks on how his heart sang as he turned from the Old Testament to the New, and came eventually to John 3:16. As he began to dwell on that great and wonderful text, he said: 'It burst upon me like a ray of sunshine in the darkness. It magnetised my soul as I pondered it.'

FURTHER STUDY

Deut. 7:6–9;
10:12–22;
John 15:9–17

1. In what ways did God demonstrate His love for Israel?

2. Catch the rhythm of God's love in Jesus.

Why does the love of God seemingly come across in the New Testament with much greater force than in the Old Testament? I think it might be because God's love could not be understood in all its fullness until humanity looked into the face of Jesus. Here humanity is at the end of its search to discover what is behind all that God does. Jesus drew back the curtains and revealed what is in the heart of God the Father. He is unconditional, unquenchable, unsearchable, undying, unutterable love.

Father, I am so thankful that You have revealed in Jesus the fullness of Your love. Help me today to live in Your unconditional, unquenchable, unending love. In Jesus' name. Amen.

A year of hope

'*There is no one, no life, no story that is beyond God's power to love and transform into renewal... God wants a relationship with each and every one of us, whoever we are, wherever we have come from, and whatever we have done or left undone.*'
– Justin Welby, Archbishop of Canterbury, in his foreword to *40 Stories of Hope*

Last Easter, CWR launched an exciting partnership project with Prison Hope, supplying thousands of prisoners with *40 Stories of Hope* – a collection of testimonies from prisoners, ex-offenders and prison chaplains who had encountered the powerful and life-changing love of Jesus. One year later, we're excited to report on how the book has been received so far, and to invite you once again to share in, and pass on, the amazing gift of hope.

Over 15,000 copies have now been sold, and 15,000 funded copies have been sent to prisoners in the UK. Though *40 Stories of Hope* was originally produced as a Lent resource, it has proven to be popular all-year round:

'*the prisoners are telling other prisoners to read it... I've been a prison chaplain for about 20 years and I learnt a long time ago that when books appear, we should order the maximum amount, as prison is like a bottomless pit and books go out*

HOPE

of print. But the demand is always there, and the story is ALWAYS the same: God's redeeming power of forgiveness. Someone tried to tell me that it's a Lent book (I know it is), but only about 20–30 people will attend Lenten groups, so I said, "No, get the books into the hands of the prisoners NOW!" Some prisoners can't wait.'

One CMS Mission Partner working in an English-speaking prison ministry in Lima, Peru, is using the book for weekly group studies with prisoners and ex-offenders. She said:

'The majority of the women that we work with are/ have been on cocaine smuggling charges, so Lee's story really struck a chord with them. One woman who normally doesn't concentrate during our Bible studies was captivated – we've never seen her concentrate so hard.'

40 Stories of Hope has been reprinted in time for Lent this year, and we are thrilled to be able to continue to supply readers both in and out of prison with these amazing stories of redemption. You can read it yourself or together with your small group, or you can buy a box of 20 books to donate to a prison. For more details, visit **cwr.org.uk/hope**

Simple – but sublime

FOR READING & MEDITATION – 1 JOHN 4:13–21

'God is love. Whoever lives in love lives in God, and God in him.' (v16)

Some may say that to talk only of God's love implies that we should never talk about God's justice, holiness and righteousness. If that is what you think I am saying then let me assure you again that it is not. Forgive me if I seem to be labouring the point but it is important, I believe, that the primary emphasis when sharing the gospel is always to show that the motive behind everything God does is love. Over the years, whenever I have spoken on the righteousness, holiness and justice of God, I have sought to explain that these attributes of the Almighty are kept in perfect balance by His everlasting love.

FURTHER STUDY

Hosea 14:1–9;
Eph. 3:14–21

1. According to Hosea, how does God love us without overlooking our sin?

2. How great is God's love, according to Paul?

In the verse before us today, the apostle John tells us that God is love. It is such a simple statement – yet so sublime. Often, however, its sublimity is missed. Think of it in this way: John does not say God has love or that God is loving. He simply says God is love. If a human being is devoid of love, he or she is still a human being, though of course a lesser being than God designed. God, however, can do nothing without love being the driving force behind His actions.

But can this love be reconciled with the fact of hell? Yes, it can. Over the past days we have been thinking about John 3:16. It is important to notice that John says, 'God so loved the world that he gave his one and only Son, that whoever believes in him shall not perish'. His love is directed towards saving us from hell. God, because He is righteous, has to administer justice, but His love led Him to ensure that men and women can escape the consequences of His justice by accepting that Christ died on the cross in their place.

God, how amazing all this is. The more I consider it, the more my soul wants to sing 'How great Thou art'. Great in power, great in holiness, great in justice, but great also in love. Glory be to Your wonderful name. Amen.

'Our gods do not love'

FOR READING & MEDITATION – JUDE 17–25

'Keep yourselves in God's love as you wait for... eternal life.' (v21)

Yesterday I mentioned that whenever I speak on such issues as the righteousness, justice and holiness of God, I am always careful to explain that the heart of the Eternal God is love. Some evangelists claim that what unconverted men and women need to hear is that they have broken the law of God and are accountable to Him for their sins. I would agree wholeheartedly but, as John Wesley said about his own preaching, 'First I preach the law and then I sprinkle it with grace.' The grace, mercy and love of God must be taught alongside His justice and righteousness if a fully orbed presentation of the gospel is to be made.

Hans Egede, one of the first missionaries to Greenland, landed in 1722 to preach the message of law and judgment: 'We must prepare these poor, degraded people,' he said, 'before they can be Christians. We must bring them to a certain state of knowledge, and then they can understand the principles of Christianity, but there is no use preaching to them as they are in this degradation.' He maintained this view for several years, and said when he left in 1736, 'I have spent my labour for nought.'

The man who took his place, John Beck, began to teach the people that despite their sins God loved them. The wild chieftain of one of the tribes said in amazement: 'You mean to tell me your God loves me? Our gods do not love; they hate us, and they try to kill us. Do you mean to say you have a God who loves?' John Beck talked to him about the love of God until his heart melted and he became a Christian. Later, I understand, the chief became an evangelist and brought many of his own tribe to Christ.

FURTHER STUDY

1 Thess. 1:2–10;
Philem. 4–16

1. What effect did God's love have on the Thessalonians?

2. What was the basis of Paul's appeal to Philemon?

Father, help me do what the text I have read today tells me to do and keep myself in Your love. Help me to ponder it continually, focus on it and praise You for it. In Jesus' name I pray. Amen.

The loving Father

FOR READING & MEDITATION – 1 JOHN 3:1–10

'How great is the love the Father has lavished on us, that we should be called children of God!' (v1)

'The greatest need in man,' says psychiatrist Karl Menninger, 'is the need to be loved.' My own experience in counselling leads me to the same conclusion. This is what men and women want to hear – and need to hear. Take the love of God out of the Christian message and you take the heart out of it. It's like removing the sun from the heavens.

Although, as we have been saying, all of God's attributes led Him to plan our redemption, the primary motive in sending His Son to die on a cross, I repeat, was love. One minister sums up the truth of the cross in these words: 'A loving Father humbled Himself to become in and through His only Son, flesh, sin and a curse for us, in order to redeem us without compromising His own character.' A loving Father – we must never forget that.

FURTHER STUDY

Jer. 31:3–9;
John 16:23–33

1. How did God show His heart of love for Israel?

2. How did Jesus speak of the Father's love?

There are some Christians who advocate the misguided view that the love in God's heart towards sinners was evoked only when the death of Christ had taken place and His justice was satisfied. But consider these words of Paul in Romans 5:6–8, so beautifully paraphrased by Eugene Peterson: 'He [Christ] didn't, and doesn't, wait for us to get ready. He presented himself for this sacrificial death when we were far too weak and rebellious to do anything to get ourselves ready. And even if we hadn't been so weak, we wouldn't have known what to do anyway' (*The Message*).

God did not love us because Jesus died; Jesus died because God loved us. Away with the misguided and misunderstood idea that Jesus had to die before God could love us. The heart of the Father is genuine love – a love that was not the result of the cross but the reason for it.

Gracious Father, as I look into Your heart I am amazed by what I see. Motivated by love, I'm never far from Your thoughts. You know me so well. Thank You for saving me. Amen.

Kissed by love

FOR READING & MEDITATION – COLOSSIANS 3:1–11

'Set your minds on things above, not on earthly things.' (v2)

For one last day we reflect on the truth that the motive, which led God to send His Son to die on the cross is His unconditional and everlasting love. An emphasis on God's love often provokes the question: If God loves sinners, does that mean He approves of their destructive actions and selfish attitudes? No, but He still loves them – even though He cannot condone their lifestyles.

The head of a boys' school, noted for its reputation for transforming rebellious youngsters into good citizens, said to one pupil, 'Johnny, we love you, but we don't like what you do'. In that statement, he gave a clue as to why the school had such a good reputation. He knew how to differentiate between the sin and the sinner. Similarly, God loves us even though He may not like the things we do.

I once read of a minister who was asked by a family to talk to their son who had turned his back on Jesus. He arrived one night just as the young man was returning from an evening of drinking. He tore into him, describing him as a drunken layabout without care or concern for his family, and declared him a worthless, good-for-nothing troublemaker. The young man, feeling he deserved it, sat there with his face in his hands and took the moral lashing without any attempt to defend himself. When the minister had finished, the mother got up and without a word walked over and kissed her son. He broke down and was instantly changed. Afterwards the son, telling of this turning point in his life, said that he could stand the lashing but he couldn't stand the kiss. Jesus is God's kiss of love placed upon a troubled and prodigal humanity.

FURTHER STUDY

Hosea 2:14–23;
Luke 15:17–24

1. According to Hosea, how does God love the unlovable?

2. How does the father show his love for the prodigal son?

God my Father, You astonish me with Your love. I can understand You loving the lovable, but loving the unlovable and the unloving is beyond me. Yet though I cannot understand it, I can still enjoy Your love. Thank You, Father. Amen.

The benefits of the cross

FOR READING & MEDITATION – ROMANS 8:1–8

'through Christ Jesus the law of the Spirit of life set me free from the law of sin and death.' (v2)

Having established that love was the primary reason God sent His Son to die on the cross, it is time now to turn to a consideration of the benefits which Jesus' sacrifice has procured for humankind.

The first is the liberty it gives us. In Romans 7, Paul tells us that we are slaves to sin (Rom. 7:14). This means that every human being is, in the moral sense, a slave: for who among us can stand up and say he has never committed sin? Rousseau, in *The Social Contract*, begins with the blunt assertion that 'Man is born free, and everywhere he is in chains' – this can be applied spiritually. The great mass of humankind, although enjoying physical freedom, is nevertheless in moral and spiritual chains. Although we are all created in the image of God, at the point of the Fall that image became marred, and as a result we have become self-centred and self-directed. It's as if people are trapped and bound to their marred design, unable to break free, no matter how hard we try, from its repetitive cycle of ultimate self-focus and destruction. Outwardly, men and women may appear free, but inwardly they are the subjects of repetitious attitudes and behaviours.

FURTHER STUDY

John 8:31–36; Gal. 5:1,13–18

1. What is it that sets us free, according to Jesus?

2. What does a life dedicated to God look like?

Do you remember how the slave trade came to be abolished? It did not come about by the slaves organising a revolt. Rather, the abolition of the slave trade was accomplished because in the heart of a man named William Wilberforce there burned a passion to set men free. And if you ask how it is that men and women can be set at liberty, then here is the answer: by means of the atoning death of our Lord Jesus Christ. Liberty of soul comes through the Son of God, and no other source.

Father, when I reflect on the wonder of the truth that I am a ransomed sinner, set free from the chains of sin, my words cannot adequately express my gratitude. But help me to do so through a life dedicated to You. Amen.

The importance of character

FOR READING & MEDITATION – PHILIPPIANS 3:1–11

*'that I may... be found in him, not having a righteousness of my own...
but that which is through faith in Christ' (vv8–9)*

Yesterday we said that one of the greatest benefits of Jesus' atoning death is the liberty it gives. Today we consider another benefit – the character it builds. The most important thing in life is not building a career but developing our character. Someone has said: 'Factories are not intended to make shoes, but to make men. If, in the process of making shoes, a man is degraded, better to have no factories.' Unfortunately, today's society seems less and less concerned about character, and more and more concerned about productivity. Most products survive for only a short time, perhaps for just a few months, whereas character lives on.

True character, however, is developed in co-operation with Jesus and the Holy Spirit. Paul gives us the key to this in the passage before us today by revealing how real character is developed by receiving the righteousness of Christ: 'That I may gain Christ and be found in him, not having a righteousness of my own that comes from the law, but that which is through faith in Christ.' When you accepted Jesus as Saviour two things happened. First, His righteousness was imputed to you – put down to your account. Second, the desire to live a righteous life was also imparted to you. Now, with the help of the Holy Spirit, that righteousness can be developed in you until the very nature of Jesus' character can be observed in you also.

What a wonderful thought, that not only are we covered with the gift of Christ's righteousness but also He is powerfully working in us to make us truly beautiful in character – a work that will last a lifetime and we can live as we were originally designed.

FURTHER STUDY

Eph. 4:20–28;
2 Tim. 2:22–26

1. How does Paul describe our new life in Christ?

2. What kind of character is Timothy urged to seek?

Father, please help me to be more concerned about my character than about my career, and teach me the art of living out the life You have put within me. For Jesus' sake I ask it. Amen.

'A palace stairway'

FOR READING & MEDITATION – COLOSSIANS 1:15–23

'and through him to reconcile to himself all things... by making peace through his blood, shed on the cross.' (v20)

We continue meditating on the benefits we receive from the death of Jesus on the cross. Another way in which His death benefits us is that it brings peace. War is a terrible thing. It means the slaughter of the innocent, the destruction of property and the breaking of hearts. I am saddened and appalled by the conflicts in the Middle East and in other parts of the world. These words ought to be written a mile high and set up in every nation: 'Blessed are the peacemakers' (Matt. 5:9).

The greatest peacemaker the world has seen, of course, is our Lord Jesus Christ. The purpose of His coming into the world was to make peace between men and God, and to show His followers how to live peacefully together. Listen again to the song of the angels at Bethlehem: 'Glory to God in the highest, and on earth peace to men on whom his favour rests' (Luke 2:14). The passage before us today has been described by one minister as 'the stairway into God's Palace of Peace'. Look at the first step: 'For God was pleased to have all his fulness dwell in him' (v19). The architect of peace is none other than God Himself, for Jesus was both fully God and fully man. And why did He come to earth in a human body? In order to bring peace to a sin-ravaged world: 'to reconcile to himself all things' (v20).

FURTHER STUDY

Psa. 85:8–13;
Phil. 4:4–9;
James 3:13–18

1. What is the effect of the peace of God in our lives?

2. What derives from the wisdom that comes from heaven?

We should notice that the peace Jesus died to provide was not the peace of compromise but the peace of conquest. He did battle against the devil, not in order to set up a compromise with him but to conquer him. Before we gave our lives to Jesus, peace was precarious and could evaporate. In Him, however, we have a peace that remains no matter what the circumstances.

Father, from the depths of my heart I praise You for giving me a peace that survives even the most turbulent of life's storms. All honour and glory be to Your wonderful name. Amen.

A blood covenant

FOR READING & MEDITATION – 1 SAMUEL 20:1–17

*'And Jonathan made David reaffirm his oath out of love for him,
because he loved him as he loved himself.' (v17)*

Today we consider yet another benefit that flows to us from
the cross – the confirmation of the covenant. The concept of
covenant is too big a subject to cover in just one day's reading,
but consider with me just one aspect of it: there are two parties
to a covenant.

In the ancient world sometimes two men would embark
upon what was known as a 'covenant of blood'. The two men,
desiring to deepen their friendship, or having been enemies
and wanting to make peace, would enter into a covenant that
required the spilling of their blood. Sitting down
together, one would bare his arm, cut the flesh until
the blood appeared, and the other would do the
same. Then, crossing their arms, their blood would
mingle, thus sealing their friendship and ratifying
the covenant. This action said, in effect: 'From
today forward my life is yours; your life is mine.
My enemies are yours; your enemies are mine. My
friends are yours; your friends are mine. Whatever
good or evil will come, we will share it together.'

We cannot be sure that David and Jonathan
mingled their blood at the time of their covenant,
though some commentators believe they did. In a
way, this is what Jesus has done for us. He took on Himself our
blood and our humanity, and when we become Christians His
blood, figuratively speaking, is passed into our spiritual veins.
Jesus became a partaker of our nature so that we might become
partakers of His. We are one with the Lord of glory. Our sins
were laid upon Him at Calvary and His righteousness was
placed on us. Whatever lies out there in the future, because
He is one with us, we shall share it together.

FURTHER STUDY

Matt. 26:26–30;
1 Cor. 11:23–26;
Heb. 9:11–15

1. In what
ways is the
Lord's Supper a
covenant meal?

2. Why is Jesus
the mediator of
a new covenant?

**Lamb of God, when I see how You have given Yourself to me in a
covenant of blood, my whole being wants to say, 'I give myself to
You – with nothing held back.' May it always be like this, dear Lord,
between us. Amen.**

What dignity!

FOR READING & MEDITATION – REVELATION 1:1–8

'To him who loves us... and has made us to be a kingdom and priests to serve his God and Father' (vv5–6)

Our text for today reveals another benefit that comes to us through the cross of Christ – the dignity it confers. What John is saying can, in effect, be summed up in three short statements: He loves us; He looses us; He lifts us. But it is the thought of being lifted that I want to take up now. Jesus Christ 'has made us to be a kingdom'. Other translations say that He has made us 'kings'. Don't do what many do and project this into the future, for the verb is in the past tense. The thing has been done; we are kings now. The crown is on our brows; God means us to reign over self and sin. He means us to have dominion. He means us to live like kings. Let's make sure that we do so.

FURTHER STUDY

1 Tim. 2:1–8;
2 Tim. 2:8–13;
1 Pet. 2:9–12

1. How does Paul link Jesus as a ransom with our intercession?

2. In what terms does Peter speak of the Church?

But John says also that He 'has made us to be… priests'. The mitre as well as the crown is upon our heads. The office to which God calls us is not just regal; it is priestly. We are lifted to the dignity of priesthood as well as the splendour of royalty. Consider what the function of a priest is. It is to represent the people before God, to pray for their forgiveness, to plead and prevail for their deliverance. In making us priests, God wants us to represent the world before Him, in prayer to bear its sorrows and carry them in compassionate, believing intercession before the throne of grace.

What great dignity Jesus has conferred upon us by lifting us from the mire of sin, putting upon us a robe of righteousness, placing upon our heads a golden crown and giving us the privilege of priestly access before His throne. Are you feeling undervalued and unappreciated? Then lift up your head. God has anointed you as priest and king!

Father, it is such a wonderful privilege to be Your child, but to be told I am also a priest and a king almost blows my mind. Is there no end to Your love and trust? Thank You, dear Father. Please help me live out my calling today. Amen.

Blood-bought victory

FOR READING & MEDITATION – REVELATION 12:1–11

'They overcame him by the blood of the Lamb and by the word of their testimony' (v11)

Now we look at another benefit of the cross – the victory it gains. Sin, we should remember, originated not in the Garden of Eden but in heaven. Satan became obsessed with a desire to take God's place, and as a result was cast out of heaven. Sin had its origin in that original rebellion. When Adam and Eve were created in the Garden of Eden, Satan came into that garden determined to destroy the creation God had made. From that day to this, Satan has been the arch enemy of the human race, bent on turning creature against Creator.

The cross, however, has ended Satan's power over humanity and has equipped us with three mighty weapons by which we can overcome him: the blood of the Lamb, the word of our testimony, and the sacrificial spirit of the cross (also spoken of in verse 11). To overcome him and walk in liberty, peace and righteousness, Satan's accusations are all met by the blood of Christ. If Satan comes to you and tells you that you are a sinner, all you have to do is remind him of the blood of Christ and he is then unable to utter another word.

A story concerning Martin Luther tells of how the devil came to him and said: 'You are a filthy sinner. Look, here is a list of your sins.' 'Is this all?' asked Luther. 'No,' replied the devil. 'Here are many more.' Faced with this list, Luther replied to his accuser with this text: 'The blood of Jesus Christ, God's Son, cleanses from all sin.' The devil, it is said, beat a hasty retreat, but not before Luther threw an inkpot at him! It is a simple tribute to the fact that Satan has to withdraw when presented with the claims of Christ's atoning blood.

FURTHER STUDY

Luke 10:17–21; Col. 2:9–15

1. What authority did Jesus give His disciples?

2. Give thanks to God for Jesus' triumph over the enemy.

Thank You, dear Lord, that Your blood is the provision by which I can overcome Satan. May I walk in its provision this day and every day I pray. For Your name's sake. Amen.

The heaven it provides

FOR READING & MEDITATION – REVELATION 21:9–27

'The twelve gates were twelve pearls, each gate made of a single pearl.' (v21)

Afurther benefit that comes to us through the cross of Christ is the final place of peace it provides. The unbounded imagery of the book of Revelation reaches its climax in this twenty-first chapter, where John describes heaven in extremely picturesque and elaborate terms.

The most intriguing thing to me about his description of the new Jerusalem is that the way in is through 12 gates, each made of pearl. You may know that a pearl is a product of pain. The oyster sitting on the seabed is invaded by a tiny parasite or a grain of sand, and instantly the healing powers of the little mollusc are marshalled at the point of peril. In that hour of mortal danger, and only at that time, the oyster exudes a precious secretion in order to heal the wound and save its life. The result is a pearl. So a pearl, it can be said, is really the result of a wound that has been healed. If there had been no wound there would have been no pearl.

FURTHER STUDY

Eph. 2:4–10;
1 Pet. 1:3–9

1. How aware are you of being seated in the heavenly realms?

2. What does our living hope consist of?

John's imagery reminds us that the only way into the new Jerusalem is through the innocent sufferings of the Lord Jesus Christ who, on the cross, endured the crushing cruelty of our sin, and turned that pain into a pearl. Jesus told a parable about finding the 'pearl of great price' (Matt. 13:46, AV). He is that pearl.

> There was no other good enough
> To pay the price of sin;
> He only could unlock the gate
> Of heaven, and let us in.

We cannot climb those jasper walls of the new Jerusalem. We can only go in through a gate. And each gate is a pearl.

Father, I am so thankful that I already belong to Your kingdom and that heaven is my final place of peace. Help me to view death not as the end but as a new beginning. In Jesus' name. Amen.

Teaching for life, faith and ministry

CWR SUMMER SCHOOL New for 2019!

At CWR, our passion is to see people encounter God in new ways, and invest in their daily walk with Him. Alongside our daily Bible reading notes, publications and church programmes, we are continually developing our range of courses and events.

We run regular short courses, such as our Introduction to Biblical Care and Counselling (IBCC), and also introduce new courses throughout the year, from Inspiring Women to Bible Discovery. We are also very excited to be re-introducing our week-long Summer School this year!

'Very valuable experience. I feel better equipped to live my Christian life.'
IBCC course delegate

'The teaching was just what I needed and the beauty of the surroundings made it even more wonderful.'
Inspiring Women course delegate

Courses can be day, evening or week-long. Whether your heart is for pastoral care, leading small groups, mentoring, delving deeper into the Bible or helping and counselling others, we hope that our courses will encourage you in your spiritual growth.

CWR Summer School

Sun–Sat, 14–20 July

An excellent opportunity for those in the UK or overseas to stay at Waverley Abbey House and attend some of our key courses and seminars all in one go!

Join us this July for a wide range of life-transforming teaching from CWR tutors Mick and Lynette Brooks, Philip Greenslade, Bob Stradling, Andy Peck and others, as well as guest contributors including Carl Beech. Choose from the dynamic range of teaching sessions topics such as:

· Christ Empowered Living
· Great Chapters of the Bible
· Spiritual Direction
· Mental Health and the Church
· Bringing the Bible to Life
· Mentoring
… and many more!

As well as engaging seminars, there will be plenty of time for rest and relaxation, and lots of other wonderful activities on offer including:

· Choir workshop with a professional choir leader
· Communion in the Abbey ruins
· Worship and devotional times
· A celebratory evening banquet
· Bread making
· A BBQ in the grounds
· Fellowship with the CWR team
... and much more!

For more information, visit
cwr.org.uk/summerschool

BOOK YOUR PLACE NOW!

Full programme runs from Monday 15 July – Saturday 20 July
Full week ticket price: **£575**
Two and three-day ticket options, non-residential options, and early bird discounts are also available.

For more information and to book, call **01252 784719**
or visit **cwr.org.uk/summerschool**

CWR short courses and seminars

One-day courses and residential courses for you, your small group or a group from your church covering Bible Discovery, Life and Discipleship, Pastoral Leadership, Small Groups, and Insight Days.

SHORT RESIDENTIAL COURSES

Take a few days out to learn, recharge, refresh and relax.

Bible Discovery Weekends

Renowned Bible teacher Phillip Greenslade spends a weekend exploring chapters of the Bible, helping you to grasp the bigger picture of God's story.

Fri–Sun, 8–10 March
Fri–Sun, 14–16 June
Fri–Sun, 6–8 September

For more information and to book, visit
cwr.org.uk/courses

Inspiring Women Courses

These courses are designed especially for women and offer opportunities for rest, reflection, solid teaching, worship and fellowship.

Fri–Sun, 15–17 March: **Free to Be**
Fri–Sun, 21–23 June: **Crowned with Honour**
Fri–Sun, 20–22 September: **Belonging**
Mon–Fri, 7–11 October: **Woman to Woman** (five-day training course)

For more information and to book, visit
cwr.org.uk/women

A wide range of evening, one-day and two-day courses are also available.
Check for details of all our courses on the website.

All courses and dates correct at time of printing and may be subject to change.

The effects of the atonement

FOR READING & MEDITATION – 2 PETER 1:1–11

'But if anyone does not have [these qualities], he... has forgotten that he has been cleansed from his past sins.' (v9)

Before we leave the subject that has been occupying our attention over recent days – the benefits that come to us through Christ's cross – I would like to spend a few days focusing on the thoughts of one of the great Welsh preachers of the past – Dr Cynddylan Jones. In his book *The Meaning of Christ's Death*, he says that there are three effects of the atonement, the first of which is redemption from what we have done in the past. Pause with me for a few moments on the truth that when we become a Christian, the past is fully and freely forgiven. One of the greatest hindrances to spiritual growth is a haunting sense of past failure and shame. Can we really be delivered from the bondage of the clinging past?

A young boy was asked by his Christian father to drive a nail into a piece of wood every time he did something wrong. Some weeks later the father went out into the garden accompanied by his small son and told him to pull out the nails one by one, confessing to what he had done wrong. After his father had forgiven him for each of his wrongs the little boy said triumphantly, 'Hooray, all the nails are gone.' 'Yes,' said his father, 'but the marks made by the nails are still in the wood.' Taking him into his garden workshop he filled the holes and planed the piece of wood until all the nail marks had gone.

That little boy never forgot the lesson his father taught him, and later in life, when he became an evangelist, his telling of that story helped thousands to realise that God will, if we let Him, remove every sense of haunting guilt and failure. But remember, only if we let Him.

FURTHER STUDY

Isa. 6:1–7;
1 Cor. 6:9–11;
Heb. 10:10–18

1. How were the Corinthians redeemed from their past?

2. How does Jesus atone for our guilt?

Lord Jesus, if I am still haunted by guilt because of some sins in my past, then help me surrender that sense of shame right now. Remove it from my soul. In Your all-prevailing name I pray. Amen.

The beat of a different drummer

FOR READING & MEDITATION – JAMES 1:19–27

*'Religion that God our Father accepts as pure and faultless is this...
to keep oneself from being polluted by the world.' (v27)*

Yesterday we referred to the lesson a Christian father taught his little boy, namely that the Carpenter of Nazareth not only forgives the past but wipes it out. This does not mean that our sin will not have consequences, but the sting and the shame are gone.

Consider now the second effect of the atonement outlined by Dr Cynddylan Jones – freedom from the prevailing influences of this present world. The society in which we live is strange, because when we fall beneath its standards, it punishes us, but when we rise above its standards, it persecutes us. 'Society,' as someone has observed, 'demands a grey, dull, average conformity.' Since a Christian is on a journey upward, he or she can quickly get out of step. Henry Thoreau, the American writer, said that when someone does not keep in step with their friends, it may be because he 'hears the beat of a different drummer'. A Christian can be described as someone who hears a different Drummer; they're no longer an echo but a voice, no longer dictated to by society but free from it. This does not mean that we run away from society, but we permeate it more deeply.

The day after I became a Christian, I announced to my friends who worked with me in the engineering shop that there were certain activities I would no longer take part in. Once I made this stand I was free, and then more able, to contribute to their lives. Many are bound by what others think of them, and live by what others are doing. A Christian is someone who has been liberated from all that and has been set free. We may be surrounded by society, but we need not be dominated by it.

FURTHER STUDY

Rom. 12:12–21;
13:8–14;
Titus 2:11–13

1. Contrast the armour of light and the deeds of darkness.

2. What does God's grace teach us to say 'yes' to and 'no' to?

Gracious and loving Lord, my different Drummer, help me to walk to the beat of Your drum and not the relentless drumming of the world that I hear all about me. In Jesus' name I pray. Amen.

Self! Self! Self!

FOR READING & MEDITATION – 2 CORINTHIANS 5:11–21

'And he died for all, that those who live should no longer live for
themselves but for him who died for them' (v15)

We look now at the third of the effects that Dr Cynddylan Jones identified as coming from the atonement – one that is made clear in our text for today: deliverance from self-centred preoccupation. There can be little doubt that one of the major problems of the soul is self-centredness. Most of us, if we are really honest, will confess that far too often it is all self, self, self.

The story is told of a French valet who was an ardent follower of communism. One day he decided to leave the communist party. In an attempt to persuade him to rejoin the party, one of the officials went looking for him and questioned him about his decision to relinquish his membership. Explaining his actions, the valet said that what caused him to renounce communism was the announcement that when the country was ruled by the communists and the wealth divided equally, each person's share would be 5,000 francs. 'Why should that make you want to leave the Communist party?' he was asked. 'Well,' he said, 'I already have 10,000 francs.'

FURTHER STUDY

Rom. 14:9–12; Phil. 2:1–11

1. For what reason did Christ die?

2. How is Christ Jesus to be our example?

Human fallenness is basically human selfishness. We hunger for attention, clamour for compliments, thrive on flattery. The Bible doesn't say self-love is wrong, but God's design is that we love Him first and that we love our neighbour as we love ourselves (Lev. 19:18; Matt. 22:37–39). Sin reverses that: we put ourselves first, before our neighbours, and God last.

Jesus' death on the cross overcomes our self-centredness without violating self. The self is freed from itself and is joined to the one who hung upon the cross. It is only when we are delivered from ourselves that we are free to give ourselves to others.

Father, I am so thankful that the cross does not bypass my central need – the need to be rescued from myself. Help me today to live less for myself and more for You and others. In Jesus' name. Amen.

A pain or a possibility?

FOR READING & MEDITATION – GALATIANS 2:11–21

'I have been crucified with Christ and I no longer live, but Christ lives in me.' (v20)

I want to spend one more day discussing the need to be set free from the problem of self. It may be because among the thousands who read these notes some will be struggling, particularly with this problem.

In the centre of the word 'SIN' is the letter 'I'. The liberty which the cross effects includes liberty from the 'I'. In today's text Paul tells us, 'I have been crucified with Christ and I no longer live, but Christ lives in me.' He goes on to say, 'The life I live in the body, I live by faith in the Son of God.' Here was an 'I' crucified yet still alive, a self fundamentally denied yet fundamentally affirmed. He then adds, 'who loved me and gave himself for me'. To do what? Among other things, to deliver me from the 'I'. Not just to save me from hell and enable me to reach heaven but to save me from the centre of my troubles – myself, the 'I'.

FURTHER STUDY

Rom. 14:13–23;
2 Cor. 8:7–9;
9:10–15

1. What kind of life pleases God?

2. How does Jesus inspire us to give?

The writer Dorothy Sayers said that there is no greater hell than to be consumed by oneself. In fact she described the hell, which is in the hereafter as 'the enjoyment of one's own way for ever'. Self in our hands is a pain; in God's hands it is a possibility. The cross, if we allow its power to penetrate our lives, can save us from ourselves and fill us with concerns for Christ and others rather than ourselves. One minister describes the surrender of the self fully into the hands of Jesus as an 'operation without anaesthetics'. He says: 'A sharp pain of penitence goes through you, then you look up into that dear Face that bends over you and you walk forth from the operating room free from that cancerous "I" and now free to live with an "I" that is Christ-centred and therefore contributive.'

Lord God, I offer myself into Your hands for whatever operation is necessary. Root out the malignancy of 'I' that is within me and make me a more contributive person. In Jesus' name. Amen.

The divine secret

FOR READING & MEDITATION – LUKE 2:41–52

'"Why were you searching for me?" he asked. "Didn't you know I had to be in my Father's house?"' (v49)

When did Jesus first come to understand that He was the promised Messiah and would end His earthly life by being strung up on a cross? Was it something that came to Him suddenly in a momentary flash of divine revelation? Or did it dawn upon Him gradually over weeks, months or even years? We can only speculate, but while we are here on earth we will never fully know.

Jesus would have been familiar with the Old Testament Scriptures in the years before His Bar Mitzvah, held on a boy's thirteenth birthday, when he became a 'son of the law'. As He became familiar with the Scriptures, the Spirit probably revealed to Him that He was the one of whom the prophets spoke. Certainly when we see Him conferring with the teachers in the Temple at the age of 12, He already appears to have been aware that He was to do His Father's work. The New King James Version highlights this by translating today's text in this way: 'Did you not know that I must be about my Father's business?' And what was His Father's business? Making it possible for lost sinners to be reconciled to Himself.

FURTHER STUDY

Luke 19:10;
John 17:1–5;
Heb. 10:1–10

1. How does Jesus describe His Father's business when He prays?

2. Why did the Son of Man come?

What would you give for a recording of Jesus' conversation with the teachers on that momentous occasion? I think I would give a great deal. What an extraordinary time it must have been in His young life. Carefully and sensitively, the Spirit had brought home to Him the truth that He was the incarnate Son of God and had come into the world to give His life as a ransom for many. The Bible treats the matter as if it is a divine secret, hence we must be careful not to speculate too deeply into a matter on which the Scriptures are so silent.

Father, on this matter we can but wonder. However, our hearts are filled with gratitude that You put together such an amazing rescue plan. All praise be to Your holy name for ever. Amen.

The Messianic secret

FOR READING & MEDITATION – MARK 8:27–33

'He then began to teach them that the Son of Man must suffer many things... and that he must be killed' (v31)

Whenever and however the truth came to Jesus that He was to die upon a cross, it is clear from the Gospels that by the age of 30, He knew that He would die a humiliating and painful death in Jerusalem (see Luke 3:23). Today's passage makes that truth very plain. Commentators view this passage as a watershed in Jesus' public ministry and say it is 'the first prediction of His passion'.

Having withdrawn with His disciples to the northern district around Caesarea Philippi, Jesus asks this challenging question: 'Who do people say I am?' (v27). When Peter blurted out, 'You are the Christ [the Messiah]', Jesus warned them not to reveal this to anyone else. He probably gave this warning for two reasons: first, because He did not want His Messianic role to be revealed until His true character had been made known (the popular Messianic expectation was that of a political leader), and second, because He wanted the revelation to be carefully unfolded by Himself.

FURTHER STUDY

Matt. 9:9–15;
Mark 9:2–13;
John 10:10–17

1. What is written about the Son of Man?

2. What was Jesus' aim in coming to this world?

Jesus began to explain some of the details about His death, warning He would be rejected by the elders, chief priests and teachers of the law, be killed, and after three days he would rise again from the dead. When Peter heard this he was outraged and remonstrated with Jesus. But Jesus turned and said to Peter that his attempt to divert Him from going to the cross was prompted by Satan. So deeply was Jesus committed to His Messianic mission that He would not allow anything to divert Him. He had not come into the world simply to teach and work miracles, wonderful though those aspects of His work were. He had come to die – for only through His death could we be given life.

Father, none of us know when we will die, where we will die or how we will die. Your Son knew all this so clearly and kept moving towards His death, aware that without His death we would never have life. My gratitude knows no bounds. Amen.

A determined mindset

FOR READING & MEDITATION – MARK 9:14–32

'But they did not understand what he meant and were afraid to ask him about it.' (v32)

Yesterday we looked at what some commentators believe to be the first clear prediction made by Jesus of His death on the cross. Today we examine the second prediction of His crucifixion. Here Jesus gives a little more detail concerning His death and makes known that He would be betrayed into the hands of men – the first intimation of betrayal.

Although the words Jesus used when describing His death are similar to the ones we looked at yesterday, this time the disciples appear not to have fully understood the import of what He was saying. They sensed, I suspect, enough, however, to realise that it was a painful subject and so did not question Him further. Matthew adds: 'And the disciples were filled with grief' (Matt. 17:23). The first time Jesus talked about His death, the disciples did not appear to be very much grieved. Was the disciples' grief now caused by this confirmation by Jesus of His earlier prediction of His death, which had brought home to them the fact that this was really going to happen? Most probably. One commentator suggests, however, that the grief which arose within them was not sympathy for Jesus and concern about His death – but was rather caused by the realisation that He would not, as they expected, end the Roman occupation and usher in the kingdom of God. If that were so, then they were thinking more of their own feelings than His.

Whatever the reason for the disciples' grief – and the first is probably more likely – we are watching a Saviour so committed to giving His life for us on a cross that He moved towards it with as much determination as any competitive athlete focuses on the finishing line.

FURTHER STUDY

Luke 9:51–62; Acts 20:17–24

1. How does Jesus indicate His determined mindset?

2. How does Paul indicate his determination to serve Jesus?

Father, the more I consider how committed Your Son was to going to the cross for my sins, the more amazed I am. May His determination to save me be matched by my determination to serve Him. Amen.

A growing fear

FOR READING & MEDITATION – MARK 10:32–34

'They were on their way up to Jerusalem... and the disciples were astonished, while those who followed were afraid.' (v32)

We find in the passage before us today yet another of Jesus' predictions of His death, and this time He actually names the city in which He is to die. Mark's account of the incident shows how the fear and astonishment that had gripped the disciples earlier was still filling their hearts: 'and as they followed they were afraid' (v32, NKJV).

Even an impartial reader of Mark's Gospel must be impressed by Jesus' steadfast determination to press on towards His final hours and death upon a cross. Some may describe this determination as a 'death wish', but as His ordeal in Gethsemane shows, He did not wish to die. He said to His close disciples: 'My soul is overwhelmed with sorrow to the point of death'. He then withdrew and prayed: '*Abba*, Father... everything is possible for you. Take this cup from me. Yet not what I will, but what you will' (Mark 14:34,36).

FURTHER STUDY

Isa. 42:1–4;
Luke 13:22,
31–35

1. What qualities does the Servant of the Lord display?

2. Why was Jerusalem Jesus' goal?

Our Lord's three predictions of His impending death on the cross contained in Mark's Gospel are thought by some commentators to be Mark's way of preparing his readers, as Jesus prepared the Twelve, for the terrible events that would end His life. In total, the Gospels record at least ten predictions, which Jesus made of His death, but the three that we have looked at over the past few days are enough to give us a clear picture of His absolute commitment to fulfilling the mission for which He came into the world. However horrible the thought of death may be to us, it would have been infinitely more horrible to Jesus because His death involved Him in bearing the sins of the whole world. As unthinkable as it was, He resolutely walked towards the cross.

Father, the more I become aware of the determination of Your Son to give His life for me, the more I long to have that same steadfastness of purpose in my own life. Help me dear Father. In Jesus' name. Amen.

The new birth

FOR READING & MEDITATION – JOHN 3:1–15

'Just as Moses lifted up the snake in the desert, so the Son of Man must be lifted up' (v14)

Over the past few days we have looked at the three predictions Jesus made concerning His death, as recorded by Mark. Now we look at one mentioned by the apostle John.

Jesus started His conversation with Nicodemus by telling him of the need for the new birth. To enter the kingdom of God, a person must receive the life of God, says Jesus. In other words, he or she must be born again. But how is this divine life brought within the reach of sinners? For the divine life to become ours, the Son of God had to die. 'Just as Moses lifted up the snake in the desert, so the Son of Man must be lifted up.' In this statement Jesus is making the point that His incarnation is not enough. His miracles are not enough. His ministry is not enough. It is His death and resurrection that brings us life.

FURTHER STUDY

Mark 12:1–12;
Luke 18:31–34;
Rom. 4:16–25

1. How does Jesus predict His death in His parable?

2. Why was Jesus delivered over to death?

The historical event Jesus refers to here is in the book of Numbers. Because of the children of Israel's grumbling and complaints against Him, God sent venomous snakes among them. When the Israelites repented, God instructed Moses to make a bronze snake and put it on top of a pole so that everyone could see it. Anyone bitten by a snake who looked at it would then live (Num. 21:4–9). And so it was.

The point to notice is this: the cure was similar to the disease. It was a snake that made the people ill and it was a snake that made them well. Here we see a glimpse of a truth that Paul later enlarged upon when he said, 'God made him who had no sin to be sin for us' (2 Cor. 5:21). Christ became our sin in order that He might become our salvation. It is a thought we should never tire of considering, for had it not been so, then our eternal destiny would have been quite different.

Lord God, may the repetition of this great truth never become dull. Rather, may the wonder of it light up my soul every time I think of it. In Jesus' name. Amen.

CWR around the world...

... from Waverley to Cambodia and beyond!

We are really starting to see CWR's ministry take root and grow in Asia and beyond. Steve Bradley, director of CWR Asia, brings us this update.

Translation of CWR publications

Our publication *Your Personal Encourager* (YPE) has been translated and is now available in Mandarin, Tamil, Telugu, Hindi, Khmer and Farsi. We have been blessed by hearing from leaders that the Farsi resource is really encouraging and helpful to the people they minister to. We are now in the process of translating into ten more languages, including Malaysian, Burmese and Nepalese, enabling the application of God's Word to reach more and more people throughout Asia.

What's even more exciting is that *YPE* is just the beginning. We have developed a full programme including *Every Day with Jesus for New Christians*, *Understanding Discipleship*, and *Growing in Discipleship* – which covers 12 key discipleship topics, with two months' focus on each. We have started translating these resources into Mandarin, Khmer, Tamil, Telugu and Hindi.

Western social media sites (such as Facebook and Twitter) are not permitted in China, but China has its own versions called WeeChat and Sina Weibo. We were very encouraged when the United Bible Society, based in Singapore, requested *Every Day with Jesus One Year Bible* (without Bible verses) to be translated and put out daily through their app, Bible Moments, on China's heavily censored internet.

Training

Our 'Care and Counselling' training has been running in Singapore for over a decade now, and in 2016 God opened a door for us to start running courses in Phnom Penh, Cambodia. Cambodia's recent history means that there are many people who have suffered great loss and trauma, with child and adult slavery being the latest battle – so we can see clearly why God has opened the door at this time. The need is huge with so many hurting people. The training has previously been run in English, but we now have training manuals in both English and Khmer, and the local team are conducting the training in Khmer, to reach a larger number of people in the country.

We plan to install new video equipment at Waverley Abbey House to enable us to record and stream conferences and courses held there. We are really excited at the prospect of streaming our courses live around the UK and the rest of the world.

Prison ministry

We continue to distribute 6,500 copies of *Every Day with Jesus* into Australian prisons six times a year, and we have had a further 500 requested – so that's 42,000 copies, reaching 7,000 prisoners with the application of God's Word daily.

We would love to ask you to join us in praying for all that God is doing around the world. If you want to donate to our ongoing work in Asia and beyond, please visit **cwr.org.uk/donate**

The Passover Lamb

FOR READING & MEDITATION – JOHN 6:25–51

'I am the bread of life. He who comes to me will never go hungry'
(v35)

Now we think about another indication Jesus gave of His death on a cross, again recorded by John, this time in the famous discourse in which Jesus referred to Himself as 'the bread of life'. This address took place at Capernaum the day after the miracle of the feeding of the 5,000. Many who were in that large crowd had followed Him to Capernaum hoping, no doubt, for a repeat of that great miracle. In response to their appeal for free bread such as their ancestors had in the wilderness, Jesus replied that He is the true bread. He then went on to make this amazing statement: 'the bread that I will give is my flesh, which I will give for the life of the world' (v51, AV).

FURTHER STUDY

Mark 14:12–24;
John 1:19–36

1. How does the Lord's Supper differ from the Passover?

2. Meditate on the significance of Jesus as the Lamb of God.

What prompted Him to make this startling statement? The explanation, I believe, can be seen in the fourth verse of this chapter: 'The Jewish Passover Feast was near.' Considering the point raised by the crowd concerning the manna provided in the wilderness, and in the atmosphere of the Passover itself, Jesus' mind would naturally have turned to the night of the Exodus. After the blood of the sacrificed lamb was sprinkled on the doorposts, each family ate the flesh (Exod. 12:8–11). Jesus knew that His death was the true fulfilment of the sacrifice that the Passover Lamb pointed to.

His death would avert the horror of sin's judgment – eternal death – and His flesh would give new life and strength to those who would receive Him and follow Him. The full meaning of these words was not fully understood by the people, nor even by the disciples, but in His own heart He saw quite clearly the event awaiting Him at Golgotha.

Quietly, dear Lord, I am entering into the pain You bore even before those nails of the cross were hammered into Your hands. And again I am overwhelmed at the wonder of Your steadfast love. Thank You, dear Saviour. Amen.

The coming of the Greeks

FOR READING & MEDITATION – JOHN 12:20–33

'Now my heart is troubled, and what shall I say? "Father, save me from this hour"? No' (v27)

Another event that caused Jesus to speak quite clearly of His impending death (again recorded by the apostle John in today's passage) was 'the coming of the Greeks'. When Jesus heard from Andrew and Philip that some Gentiles wished to see Him, He began to talk about His glorification in death and said that His heart was 'troubled'. The Greek text indicates a deep disturbance of spirit.

We do not know exactly what was in the minds of the Greeks in wanting an audience with Jesus. Perhaps they intended to invite Him to come to their own country and add His philosophy to the multiplied philosophies of the day. Greece was well known for its high regard for philosophers. However, although we do not know what was in the mind of the Greeks, I think we can know what was in the mind of Jesus – the thing that caused His soul to be troubled. Jesus came to bring His message to the nation of Israel. He knew, through the Spirit, that He would be rejected by His own people, and that after His sacrificial death, the offer of salvation would be extended and opened up to the Gentiles.

FURTHER STUDY

John 4:39–42; 10:14–18; Rev. 5:6–10

1. What was the Samaritans' testimony?

2. How does John see Jesus drawing all men to Himself?

My own thinking on this matter leads me to the conclusion that the visit of the Gentiles underlined this truth in His mind and brought even more closely to Him the reality of His death upon a cross. He sensed the time was swiftly approaching when He would open up a path for men and women of every race to find salvation. The statement He made immediately following their visit would seem to indicate that this was so: 'But I, when I am lifted up from the earth, will draw all men to myself' (v32). The cross was now nearer than ever.

Blessed Lord Jesus, sometimes, because I know You are the Son of God, I forget You are also the Son of Man. You bore the agony of Your anticipated death, not for any benefit You would gain, but for me. I am so very, very thankful. Amen.

A momentous walk

FOR READING & MEDITATION – LUKE 9:28–36

'They spoke about his departure, which he was about to bring to fulfilment at Jerusalem.' (v31)

For one more day we consider Jesus' own awareness of the fact that He was destined to die on a cross. When we consider that He had the right to return to heaven without dying, how grateful we can be that He went back to heaven by way of the cross.

I have selected the story of the Transfiguration for our reading today so that we can focus particularly on these words: 'They spoke about his departure.' The Greek word Luke uses to speak of Jesus' departure is *exodus*. How fascinating that conversation Moses and Elijah had with Jesus must have been. Moses had died, I imagine, with a degree of sadness in his heart, as he was unable to complete the work of bringing the people he had led for 40 years into the Promised Land (see Deut. 34). When Elijah was taken to heaven in a chariot of fire (see 2 Kings 2:1–12), the people of Israel were still participating in the worship of the pagan god Baal. These men did their work and laid it down unfinished. God, however, gathered them into the glory of His kingdom and allowed them to return to earth to talk to the One who would complete the work that was yet unfinished.

FURTHER STUDY

John 17:6–14;
18:4–11

1. Just before His death, how did Jesus pray?

2. In the shadow of the cross, what attitude did Jesus display?

Through His work on the cross, Jesus accomplished an exodus far greater than anything Moses was involved in. He has freed not just a nation from physical servitude, as Moses did. Instead He has released multiple billions from spiritual captivity and set them down in what the apostle Paul describes as the 'glorious freedom of the children of God' (Rom. 8:21). Bearing in mind what I have said, the walk from the Mount of Transfiguration to the hill called Calvary must figure as the most momentous walk ever undertaken.

Lord Jesus Christ, I am so grateful that You took that walk from the Mount of Transfiguration to the hill of Calvary. Because of what You did, heaven's door is open to me. Thank You, dear Lord. Amen.

The cosmic cross

FOR READING & MEDITATION – REVELATION 13:1–9

'the Lamb… was slain from the creation of the world.' (v8)

We move on now to consider the thought that before the cross was an act in time, it was a fact in eternity. The death of Jesus Christ was not an accidental occurrence – something that simply happened by chance in an obscure corner of the Roman Empire. It was planned by God before the earth was even created. According to the text before us today, Jesus was the Lamb slain from the creation of the world. But exactly what does that mean?

This verse, understandably, puzzles a great many people. During my pastoral days, when I was leading a Bible study on Revelation 13, someone in the group said concerning today's text, 'I thought Jesus was killed 2,000 years ago on a hill just outside the walls of Jerusalem, so how can He be said to have been slain from the creation of the world?' Here, I believe, is the answer: when God created the world and established the universe He foresaw the chaos that would enter His creation and prepared for it by planning our redemption. This means that in the mind of God, the cross was not an afterthought but something carefully considered and planned before the world was made. There was a cross in the heart of God aeons before there was one set up on the hill called Calvary.

The awe-inspiring act of atonement took place in time, but clearly the cross was antedated in eternity. In a sense then, it can be said that the cross is cosmic; from the beginning of the creation its shadow has been cast over the whole universe. The cross was not something that merely came out of history; it was something that came into it. God had a Lamb before He had a man!

FURTHER STUDY

John 17:20–26; Acts 2:22–28

1. Of what was Jesus aware before the creation of the world?

2. Trace God's actions in the first part of Peter's sermon.

Father, once again I come before You with thanksgiving for the truth that the cross was not an afterthought but a forethought. You knew humanity would fall. What wondrous grace. All glory be to Your name forever. Amen.

Freedom of choice

FOR READING & MEDITATION – GENESIS 2:15–25

'You are free to eat from any tree... but you must not eat from the tree of the knowledge of good and evil' (vv16–17)

When the matter of sin being present in the universe God made is discussed, two questions are often asked, the first being this: couldn't God have made a universe in which sin is an impossibility? He could have done so, but just imagine what kind of world it would have been – a world in which we would have been like pre-programmed automatons responding to God in the same way a computer responds to someone typing the keys.

When God created the first human pair, He made them to enjoy a dependent relationship with Himself but, because they had the gift of free will, it was possible for them break that relationship through acting independently of Him. It has been said that 'God created beings with free will, and though this makes evil possible, it is the only thing that makes possible any love or goodness or joy worth having.' I might love the ability of my computer to respond instantly to my commands, but the ability to love and form a relationship with a machine is only in the realm of science fiction.

The other question that arises in connection with God allowing sin in His universe is this: couldn't God remove by a miracle the results of every wrong choice human beings make? However, if God did that then choice itself would cease to exist. Free will would be meaningless in a world where God corrected the consequences of our choices at every moment. Our wills are free: we are free to follow Him or not to follow Him. Which will we choose? Our wills are ours to make them His.

FURTHER STUDY

Deut. 30:11–20;
Prov. 16:16;
John 7:17–24

1. What choices were set before the people of Israel?

2. What did Jesus indicate would be a good choice?

Father, I see I am free either to resist You or to rejoice in You. I am so grateful for the leading of Your Spirit that has helped me to follow You. All glory be to Your wonderful name. Amen.

An expected event

FOR READING & MEDITATION – ISAIAH 53:1–12

'he was led like a lamb to the slaughter... so he did not open his mouth.' (v7)

Today we again reflect on the truth that we know the cross was not a divine afterthought because we are told Jesus was 'the Lamb… slain from the creation of the world' (Rev. 13:8). There are some who take exception to this, claiming that it was never in the mind of God for Jesus to be crucified; they believe His intention was that Jesus should be followed.

Dr Albert Schweitzer seemed to be of this opinion. The man may have been a wonderful humanitarian, but when it came to the subject of Christ and His cross, he seems to have been somewhat confused. Jesus, he once wrote, 'expected the kingdom to come during His time in Jerusalem, and when it didn't appear in the way He expected and was put on a cross, He died there of a broken heart crying, "My God, why have You forsaken me?" But in dying He left an ethic of love.' But reading the Old Testament we find many predictions of the cross. Today's reading is just one of many that point to the Lamb slain before the foundation of the world.

FURTHER STUDY

Eph. 1:3–10;
1 Pet. 1:10–12

1. What choices did God make?

2. In what ways was the cross an expected event?

Though I have told the following story before, it bears repeating. Some Christians in China who were forbidden to practise the Christian faith used to sit in a room and let the sun shine on a mirror, which was positioned in such a way that it threw an outline of the cross upon the wall. The outline drew their minds to the cross, and silently they would worship the One who gave His life for them on the tree. If someone who was not a Christian entered the room, they would simply adjust the mirror so it no longer caught the rays of the sun. The outline of the cross, reflected in the pages of the Old Testament, shows it to have been an expected event, not an unexpected one.

Loving heavenly Father, it is clear from Your Word that Your Son would be crucified, and although I may not fully understand why, I am so very grateful for His sacrifice. Amen.

Love on the line

FOR READING & MEDITATION – 1 PETER 3:8–22

'For Christ died for sins once for all, the righteous for the unrighteous, to bring you to God.' (v18)

The amazing truth that the cross has lain on the heart of God from all eternity is one of the most awe-inspiring truths to be found in Scripture. I find nothing in the annals of history more moving and wonderful than this. Imagine it – God proceeded with the act of creation, knowing all the time that one day He would have to see His Son become incarnate and watch Him being fixed to a cross. What incredible love for His creation must surge through the heart of God.

While reading Eugene Peterson's paraphrase of Romans, I came across this, which touched me deeply: 'We can understand someone dying for a person worth dying for, and we can understand how someone good and noble could inspire us to selfless sacrifice. But God put his love on the line for us by offering his Son in sacrificial death while we were of no use whatever to him' (Rom. 5:7–8 *The Message*). 'God put his love on the line for us.' How wonderful.

FURTHER STUDY

2 Tim. 1:8–12;
1 John 1:1–7

1. What was given us in Christ Jesus before the beginning of time?

2. Why did John write his epistle?

During the First World War, an officer was about to go on a dangerous mission into 'no man's land' to cut wires. He said to the chaplain, 'Pray that I might get back safely.' 'I will do more than that,' responded the chaplain. 'I will go with you.' During the expedition a shell exploded near the two men. The chaplain threw himself on the officer, saving his life, but losing his own.

This gives us some idea of what Jesus did for us on the cross. God, in the Person of His Son, came to this world, walked with humanity, and chose that the penalty of sin which should have fallen on us – that is, death – should fall upon Him instead. I don't know about you, but my response to a God who would do that is one of love and gratitude.

Lord Jesus, once again my heart rises in praise and gratitude to You for taking on Yourself the sins of the whole earth. Yours is all the honour and the glory. Amen.

In the heart of God

FOR READING & MEDITATION – 1 JOHN 2:1–14

'He is the atoning sacrifice for our sins, and not only for ours but also for the sins of the whole world.' (v2)

As we draw near to Easter, we continue reflecting on the truth that Jesus was the Lamb slain before the creation of the world.

Some years ago, when some friends and I were visiting a cathedral while on holiday, we caught sight of a large cross hanging just a few feet from the roof. But instead of being hung vertically, it was hanging horizontally. When we asked one of the vergers why this was so, he said: 'Our dean had this done to illustrate that there was a cross up there in the heart of God before there was a cross down here in time.' He continued: 'Also, as you may know, ancient cathedrals were built in the shape of a cross. The chancel and nave represent the upright of the cross and the two transepts the cross-beam. This cathedral is a cruciform structure. The cross up there mirrors the cross down here, and it is this that our dean, who is a great enthusiast for the message of the cross and who preaches on it continually, wanted to convey to those who worship here and also, of course, those like yourselves who come in to view the cathedral.' After we heard what the verger had to say, we were so moved that we knelt right there in prayer and gave thanks for the dramatic reminder that the cross was the outworking of a purpose that laid on God's heart from all eternity.

Many sermons will be preached all over the world in this season on the theme of the cross, in which preachers will say, 'Here on earth a cross has been uplifted on which our Saviour died.' But let us not forget also that in eternity past, a cross was lifted up in the heart of God – evidence of the truth that the cross was not an accident but a preordained event.

FURTHER STUDY

Rom. 8:28–32;
Eph. 1:11–14;
3:7–12;
Heb. 6:16–20

1. What did God plan, according to Paul?

2. For whom does God work for good?

Father, my heart never ceases to rejoice over the fact that the cross did not just come out of history but was part of Your design. With masterly strategy You planned my salvation. I am so very, very grateful. Amen.

The God who gave Himself

FOR READING & MEDITATION – 1 TIMOTHY 2:1–15

'the man Christ Jesus... gave himself as a ransom for all men' (vv5–6)

The great evangelist John Wesley said that he employed two tests for any teaching he gave to people: first, is it in the Bible? And second, is it discerned in experience? Clearly the cross is in the Bible, but is it discerned in experience also?

Many years ago I heard the great Welsh Bible teacher W.L. Rowlands make the point that the sacrificial spirit – which was in the heart of God as He created the universe – is reflected in the very creation He made. 'In one sense,' he said, 'the cross and the spirit of self-sacrifice is built into all creation. The seed dies that the plant may live. It is even in our blood. The white corpuscles watch for infection, and when they find it they throw themselves upon it and die, in order that the organism might live.' An intriguing, though controversial, thought. It is certainly true that the spirit of self-sacrifice is evident in life. Firemen will go into a burning building and risk their own lives in order to save others. A diver is willing to put his life on the line in order to rescue boys trapped in a cave because something deep within prompts him to do so.

FURTHER STUDY

Gen. 22:1–14;
John 12:23–26

1. How did Abraham reflect what was in God's own heart?

2. How did Jesus illustrate the spirit of self-sacrifice?

Is this spirit of self-sacrifice a reflection of the glorious, amazing truth that we are made in God's image? If it is, then the law of self-sacrifice, which is to be found in the heart of God and in the Bible, is to be found also in the very texture of human life. As I said, this is a controversial thought and I do not wish to pursue it, but I often wonder if the spirit of self-sacrifice, which has been demonstrated throughout history, is explainable by the fact that we are made in the image of God – a God who gave Himself up for others.

God my Father, is the universe not just the work of Your hands but the work of Your heart as well? It would seem so. No sacrifice, however, can be greater than Yours. You gave Your Son for me – even me. My gratitude knows no bounds. Amen.

The agony in the garden

FOR READING & MEDITATION – MATTHEW 26:36–46

'My Father, if it is possible, may this cup be taken from me. Yet not as I will' (v39)

Today is known as 'Maundy Thursday', when we remember the Lord's Supper and the other events that preceded Jesus' arrest. What a struggle must have gone on in His heart as He wrestled with the thought that soon He would be hammered to a cross. It would have been hard enough to know that He was drawing near to the hour of His death, but to contemplate the agony of both His physical and spiritual suffering must have affected Him more deeply than we can ever imagine. He was, after all, human as well as divine.

A church leader suggested that what Jesus felt in Gethsemane He had already felt to some degree, when back in eternity He accepted that one day He would become a man and die on a cross for the sins of the world. This is a great mystery, of course, and we can never fully fathom it. It confounds the angels and it confounds us also. One day we may understand it better, but not now.

Whatever feelings were in the heart of the Son in eternity, in the Garden of Gethsemane He was feeling them in His human body. One writer, when reflecting on the view that in Gethsemane Jesus came face to face with a reality that had been on His heart from eternity, said: 'As the flash of a volcano discloses for a few hours the elemental fires at the earth's centre, so the light around Calvary was the bursting forth through historical conditions of the very nature of the Everlasting.' In the agony of the garden we see bursting forth into history something not only of the burden that had been on His heart from all eternity but also of the great love for lost humanity which, like a fire, had been always burning in His heart.

FURTHER STUDY

1 Cor. 6:19–20; Heb. 5:7–10

1. How should we respond to the price that was paid?

2. What did Jesus learn from what He suffered?

Thank You, Lord Jesus, that in the face of Your great suffering, though You flinched, You did not fail. My salvation is without price, but it is not without cost. It cost You Your precious blood. I cannot thank You enough. Amen.

'Sunday's coming!'

FOR READING & MEDITATION – MATTHEW 27:57–66

'"Sir," they said, "we remember that while he was still alive that deceiver said, 'After three days I will rise again.'"' (v63)

As we come to Good Friday, consider with me once again what took place in old Jerusalem.

Working out the exact timing isn't easy, but it seems that within about 12 hours of His arrest, Jesus was on the cross. Twelve awful hours! He was examined four times by four different tribunals. He was rushed from Annas to Caiaphas, to Pilate, to Herod, and back to Pilate again. And then to the cross. There He hung in agony in the heat while abuse was hurled at Him. Through His swimming eyes He saw His mother's face. And John, faithful to the last, was at her side (John 19:26). After hours of intense pain Jesus cried, 'It is finished' (John 19:30) and, as one final act, Jesus committed His spirit into His Father's hands (Luke 23:46).

And then the tomb. Our crucified Lord was laid on a cool rock, not to await decomposition but to fulfil the purposes of God and rise again.

What a difference it would have made to the disciples if only they had believed what Jesus had told them concerning His death and resurrection. The priests and Pharisees appeared to take it seriously, as our text for today shows. For the unaware and confused disciples, the days following the crucifixion seemed to spell defeat, yet had they held on to Jesus' words, their thoughts, summed up famously by S.M. Lockridge, would have been, 'Friday's here... but Sunday's coming!' The crucified one would rise again.

If today you feel downcast and defeated, my message to you is: hold on – Sunday's coming. In God's good time the stone will be rolled away and defeat will give place to victory.

FURTHER STUDY

Psa. 16:1–11;
Luke 24:36–48

1. What assurances did the psalmist have?

2. How did Jesus reassure His disciples?

Lord God, You know the struggles I am experiencing right now. Help me to hold on to You. Let me know Your presence, strength and grace to wait in hope until the stone is rolled away. In Jesus' name. Amen.

Sin crucified God

FOR READING & MEDITATION – MATTHEW 27:32–50

'When they had crucified him, they divided up his clothes by casting lots.' (v35)

During these days when our thoughts are focused on Jesus' crucifixion, many will no doubt ponder the question of why it was necessary for Jesus to die such a cruel and traumatic death. The answer, I believe, is this: only a brutal death could have exposed sin in the way it so sorely needed exposing. A London preacher once asked: 'Could Jesus have exposed sin in all its foul horror if He had died in His bed, or by accident, or by disease?'

It is one of the tragedies of human life that we fail to recognise the gravity of sin. When speaking of sin we use such euphemisms as 'mistakes', 'faults', 'errors of thought', and so on. So what is sin? I will tell you what sin is: it is the selfishness in our nature that will take a loving God and crucify Him. That is sin. Your sin, and mine. Look at the cross and you can see, placarded before your eyes, the truth that when the self-centredness of human nature is fully expressed, it is capable of nailing God to a tree.

Have you ever looked at bacteria that cause disease under a microscope? They are extremely interesting – and sometimes beautiful. But go into a hospital ward and see them at work. The germs that look so innocent, so harmless and even beautiful, destroy human features, eat a person's living flesh away and are the cause of the most horrible deaths. You didn't realise the deadly character of the germ when you looked at it under a microscope, but when you see what it does you are forced to acknowledge its malignancy. So it is with sin. Stand at the cross and observe what it does. There, sin is seen in all its hideous foulness. A crucified Saviour reveals it.

FURTHER STUDY

Rom. 5:12–17; 6:11–18; 1 John 2:3–6

1. How does grace surpass the reality of sin?

2. Contrast being slaves to sin with being slaves to obedience.

Blessed Lord, as I contemplate Your sufferings I bow down in worship. If my sin did that to You, then how can I choose the way of sin again? Jesus, stay close to me and help me keep free from sin. For Your own dear name's sake. Amen.

Two words, two worlds

FOR READING & MEDITATION – MATTHEW 28:1-15

'He is not here; he has risen, just as he said. Come and see the place where he lay.' (v6)

Christ is risen! He is risen indeed! Today this cry will ring out all around the world as it has done for centuries. The message that exhilarated the apostle Peter on the Day of Pentecost (see Acts 2:14) is one that inspires us also: it was possible for Jesus to die, but it was not possible for Him to be held by death. In the words of John Stott, 'We live and die, Christ died and lives!' Non-Christians wonder why we make so much of the resurrection. Well, here's the reason. It was the public proclamation of the truth that Jesus' death on the cross accomplished the atonement for our sins. If Jesus had not risen from the dead, then no one would ever have a hope of their sins being forgiven and going to heaven when they die. Though it was not the resurrection alone that saved us, if there had been no resurrection then the death of Jesus would have been shown to have no saving power and we would have no access to the life of God.

FURTHER STUDY

Acts 2:29-35;
13:26-38

1. What was Peter so confident about?

2. What did Paul make so much of?

One theologian said some time ago: 'We don't have to believe in the resurrection for Christianity to be perpetuated. It will survive without it.' But would it? Perhaps it would survive as a moral philosophy, but not as a dynamic faith. We see in the passage before us today that the two Marys were surprised when they came and found the tomb empty. But imagine the effect upon them and the ages if Jesus had still lain there. As a poet has put it: 'Oh, the anguish of Mary!, O the depth of despair! Imagine if she had gone to the tomb and the dead Lord was there.' How wonderful that today we don't have to say, 'Come and see where He lies,' but, 'Come and see where He lay.' Two different words, two different worlds. Hallelujah!

Lord Jesus, I greet You on this wonderful morning – the most glorious dawn in history. That radiance casts its glow over every other dawn. Because You live, I live also. Hallelujah! Amen.

FOR READING & MEDITATION – ROMANS 12:1–11

'Therefore, I urge you, brothers, in view of God's mercy, to offer your bodies as living sacrifices' (v1)

The cross and Jesus' resurrection has forever changed the world. The question we ask ourselves now is this: do we allow the truth of Jesus' atoning death merely to remain in our minds as a doctrine or do we invite the Holy Spirit to make it a dynamic reality in our hearts?

Just before the battle of Drumclog in 1679, a Scottish preacher, Thomas Douglas, addressed a crowd of people on a hillside. Suddenly he was interrupted by the sound of a gunshot. It was the signal fired to give warning of the approaching redcoats – the dreaded English soldiers. The preacher faced his followers and said, 'You have had enough theory' (meaning they had heard his views on the need to counter the English). 'Now,' he said, 'for the practice!'

Many Christians make the mistake of supposing that when they have listened to a sermon, read a book, or followed a series of studies such as I have presented in this issue of *Every Day with Jesus*, and given mental assent to what has been said, their duty has been discharged and they may then simply dismiss the subject from their minds. That may possibly be true of some subjects, but it is certainly not true of the atonement. For the doctrine of the cross to be of any value to us, it needs to be embodied in everyday life. The doctrine becomes the deed; the learning of spiritual truth always flows into the living of a spiritual life. God wants us to take what we have learned about the cross and apply it day by day. The message that came through Jesus can now be brought alive in us. So the next few days are not the end – but the beginning. We have had the theory – now for the practice!

FURTHER STUDY

Luke 6:43–49;
Heb. 13:11–16;
James 2:14–26

1. How does Hebrews link Jesus' sacrifice with our sacrifice?

2. How does James describe faith without deeds?

Loving heavenly Father, having come so far, help me not to turn back now. Prepare me for the challenge that lies ahead in these next few days, and enable me to turn theory into practice. In Jesus' name. Amen.

FOR READING & MEDITATION – 1 CORINTHIANS 2:1–10

'I resolved to know nothing while I was with you except Jesus Christ and him crucified.' (v2)

Yesterday we made the point that when we have listened to the Word of God that is not the end but merely the beginning. It is time now to invite the Holy Spirit to help us apply what we have learned about the cross to our individual lives. And how do we do that? By recognising that the only way to look out at the universe is through the cross.

At one time in my life, I looked at the universe through eyes that had never focused on the cross, and what I saw there – suffering, pain, sickness, tragedy and death – filled me with despair. I asked myself, 'Is there any meaning or purpose in this chaotic universe? If there is a God, does He care?' I had no answer. Life seemed purposeless and pointless. Then I became a Christian and I learned to look at life differently. At the cross, I saw a God who entered our world, took my sufferings on Himself, and suffered all that I suffered – and far, far more. Now my universe holds steady. The cross saves me from pessimism and despondency by showing me that it is possible to use the pain and suffering that exists to achieve self-sacrificing and redemptive ends. The cross is light – the only light – for it shows that God can take the worst and make it into the best. He took the sin of the whole world and in one glorious act of self-sacrifice bore it all away.

FURTHER STUDY

Rom. 8:31–37;
2 Cor. 1:1–11

1. Through what lens is Paul looking at suffering and struggles?

2. From what does Paul derive light and life through suffering?

When you and I begin to learn to look at life through the cross and realise that God worked there to make it possible for sins to be forgiven, turning the worst into the best, then we can more confidently commit our lives to His all-conquering love, and in this way the principle of the cross is transposed into our lives.

Lord Jesus, I see clearly now that I can only interpret life in the light of the cross. I look through Your wounds and I see not only life but light – the light of life. Amen.

God's New Society

For over two thousand years, the Church of Jesus Christ has been changing lives and serving the world. But what are the defining characteristics of the Church that have kept it strong throughout the ages?

Following the resurrection and ascension of Jesus, God established on earth a new society, against which the gates of hell would not prevail. Join us next issue as we revisit the Early Church in the book of Acts, and re-apply some timeless principles for a thriving spiritual community.

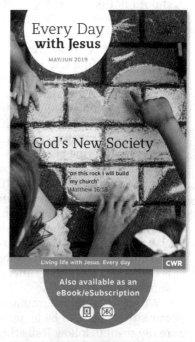

Every Day
with Jesus
MAY/JUN 2019

God's New Society

'on this rock i will build
my church'
Matthew 16:18

Living life with Jesus. Every day   CWR

Also available as an
eBook/eSubscription

A cross is inevitable

FOR READING & MEDITATION – LUKE 14:25–35

'anyone who does not carry his cross and follow me cannot be my disciple.' (v27)

We continue meditating on how we can apply what we have learned about the cross in our own lives. Another matter we embrace, as Jesus taught, is that every follower of His must be prepared to take up a cross. All Christ's disciples must be willing to deny themselves and suffer for Him. We should not be surprised that a cross will arise where our concerns and Christ's meet – and this is a great challenge. Our choice then is to decide whose concerns are to hold sway. Those who give themselves to Jesus' claims and put Him first will find that He brings us in line with His concerns. Our compassion will be widened and our capacity for suffering increased. Each new friendship we form, each new injustice we set out to correct, each new sin in others to which we expose ourselves, each new enterprise we take on for God, will become a possible suffering point.

We must simply recognise, if we are not to be overwhelmed by life, that a personal cross is inevitable. Jesus' compassion was universal in width and infinite in depth. He was the Son of Man, so the suffering that came to Him as a result of that truth was also universal and infinite. He touched all life with love, and out of that love all His being reacted in suffering. The cross is the focal point of that suffering. Jesus loved all and therefore suffered for all.

We however, are not infinite beings but finite ones. Therefore our sufferings will be lesser – but equally inevitable. If we really want to follow Jesus then we must face the fact that as we become personally and socially involved with a world of sin, a cross awaits us. It is inevitable.

FURTHER STUDY

2 Cor. 4:7–18;
1 Tim. 6:11–16

1. How did Paul identify with the cross?

2. How did Paul link Timothy's experience with that of Jesus?

Lord Jesus, I recognise that You called Your disciples to take up a cross and follow You. Strengthen me to face the inevitability of a cross. For Your own dear name's sake. Amen.

Four men who bore crosses

FOR READING & MEDITATION – 1 PETER 2:19–25

'Christ suffered for you, leaving you an example, that you should follow in his steps.' (v21)

Yesterday we said that when we take up a cross, which Jesus asks us to do, a degree of suffering and pain is inevitable. It was so in the life of Jesus and it will be so in our lives too. It is one thing, however, to see the cross as inevitable; it is another to reach out deliberately and grasp it.

Four people bore crosses on that first Good Friday. The first was Simon of Cyrene. He was compelled to carry Christ's cross (Matt. 27:32). He had no choice in the matter. Life often does that – it seizes us and puts a cross on our unwilling shoulders. Another man to bear a cross was the rebellious thief. His was a cross of burning anger. He blamed Jesus for not saving Himself and them. He died blaming everybody but himself (Luke 23:39). Some bear a cross like that – with no repentance, no reconciliation, no release. The third man to bear a cross was the penitent thief. He looked beyond the shame of it to see that Jesus really was a king (Luke 23:40–43). His cross had meaning – it began in pain and ended in peace.

The last cross was that of Jesus – a chosen cross. The rest were involuntary – His was voluntary. He could have avoided it by calling upon His Father to send 12 legions of angels to defend Him (Matt. 26:53). But instead, He willingly stretched out His hands to receive the nails of the cross and, by doing so, showed the greatest love of all. If, as we have said, a cross is inevitable in life, then don't let it be thrust upon you grudgingly and unwillingly. Anticipate it, accept it and through it, lift others. Christ's cross was a chosen cross. It is also the Christian's cross.

FURTHER STUDY

Rom. 15:1–6;
Gal. 5:22–26;
6:1–5

1. How are we encouraged to bear with the failings of the weak?

2. How should we carry each other's burdens?

Father, help me to reach out today for the cross that You are holding before me and to use it for the good of myself and others. In Jesus' name. Amen.

The Christian's joy

FOR READING & MEDITATION – HEBREWS 12:1–11

'Let us fix our eyes on Jesus... who for the joy set before him endured the cross' (v2)

Now that we have spoken of the pain that lies in the cross, we can move on to speak of its joy, for the Christian's joy is a joy won out of the heart of pain. In today's text the writer to the Hebrews urges us to 'fix our eyes on Jesus... who for the joy set before him endured the cross'. Jesus was able to bear the cross because He looked beyond it and saw what it would accomplish. And the joy of His achievement was greater than the depth of His pain.

FURTHER STUDY

Matt. 5:10–16;
Heb. 10:32–39;
James 1:2–12

1. Why should the persecuted rejoice?

2. What does James consider to be pure joy?

There are many types of joy in the world. There is the joy, which a person experiences when they triumph over a weaker individual. I once heard of a supermarket manager who boasted that his new supermarket had put three small grocery shops out of business. His was the joy of the triumph of the strong over the weak. Many sing that song. Their joy is the joy of personal advantage, no matter what it may cost others. Another side of this triumphing over weaker individuals is when someone, in climbing the ladder of selfish ambition, tramples others underfoot to reach the top. This kind of joy is, however, a superficial and short-lived joy.

The joy that endures is the joy that comes through doing good to those who ill-treat you – the joy of one who dies for his crucifiers. This is the kind of joy Jesus had, and this is the kind of joy He is able to impart to us. This word joy is so small but so rich in depth and meaning. It's difficult to capture all that it conveys: it encompasses peace and contentment, to jumping up and down in excitement. Let's look at life, then, not only through the cross but beyond the cross. There you will see joy – cleansing joy, energising joy, service-inspiring joy.

Father, thank You for showing me that the last word is not pain, but joy. And please help me not simply to adjust to the pain and suffering of this life but to contemplate the future joy. In Jesus' name. Amen.

Crucified afresh

FOR READING & MEDITATION – HEBREWS 6:1–12

'to their loss they are crucifying the Son of God all over again and subjecting him to public disgrace.' (v6)

Today's text tells us that although the crucifixion of Jesus was a unique event that took place around 2,000 years ago, there is a sense in which He is being crucified still. How is it possible for Christ to be crucified afresh? According to the writer of the book of Hebrews, it happens when those who were once enlightened and have tasted of the heavenly gift fall away and deny the faith. Such a disavowal is tantamount to once again swinging the hammers that crucified Jesus and driving the nails into His hands.

There is a difference of opinion among Bible commentators as to whether this passage relates to true Christians or 'nominal' Christians. Since the writer is referring to those who have 'tasted the heavenly gift,' some say this clearly indicates they were true Christians, especially as verse 4 speaks of sharing in the Holy Spirit, whereas others argue you can taste something without actually assimilating it.

However we interpret the passage, the issue I want to draw from this is that those who claim to be Jesus' followers and yet refuse to live as He wants us to are really denying and dishonouring Him. I am speaking metaphorically when I say this, but the Saviour bleeds again when we choose not to follow Him in all that He calls us to do and act in ways that bring dishonour to His name. Often we emphasise the suffering of Christ for the world, but what about the suffering He endures from those of us who say we bear His name and yet in that very name do so many ugly and unpleasant things? It could be said that Jesus' pain did not end when He was crucified on the cross. It continues every time we put our own interests before His.

FURTHER STUDY

Eph. 4:29–32; 1 John 2:15–23

1. What grieves the Holy Spirit?

2. Distinguish between denying the Son and acknowledging the Son.

Lord Jesus, my Saviour, forgive me for the sadness and grief I bring to You when, as Your child, I choose my way instead of Yours. I ask not only for cleansing but for the strength to be all that You want me to be in this present world. Amen.

Again He bleeds

FOR READING & MEDITATION – JOHN 19:16–24

'They divided my garments among them and cast lots for my clothing.' (v24)

Yesterday I said that although the crucifixion of Jesus was a unique event, there is a sense in which the pain of the cross continues. When we refuse to follow God's instructions given to us in the Bible, and put our own interests before His, the Saviour again bleeds. But is this taking things too far? Can it really be said that we are crucifying the Son of God afresh when we act in ways that bring dishonour to His name? Once again, it must be understood that I am speaking metaphorically here. We do not hurt Him physically but we do hurt Him by causing Him sorrow.

FURTHER STUDY

1 Cor. 5:1–8; 6:1–8; 10:14–22; 11:27–32

1. How does Paul link the cross with Christian behaviour?

2. What is the right way to participate in the Lord's Supper?

Some time ago I heard of a church building, which was taken over by the local authority and sealed, because every time the Christians who belonged to the church gathered together there, the meeting ended in a fight. There were two factions in the church who had quarrelled with each other, and each faction wanted the other group to leave the church and find another building in which to conduct their services. Several times when fights broke out (which involved women as well as men) the police were called to the church. Both factions then sought to settle the matter of the ownership of the building by going to court. You can imagine what the local newspapers made of that. When I heard that story, my mind went to the cross of Jesus and the passage that I have asked you to look at today. I thought of the soldiers who gambled for Jesus' clothes as He hung dying upon the tree – the focus of our reading today. Casting lots for His clothes and going to court to settle spiritual matters – is there any difference? In my opinion, little or none.

Lord God, my heart too is pained as I hear of the ugly things done by Your Church which perpetuate the pain of the cross. Wake us up to see that to dishonour Your name before society is to crucify You afresh. Amen.

FOR READING & MEDITATION – ZECHARIAH 13:1–9

'If someone asks him... he will answer, "The wounds I was given at the house of my friends."' (v6)

Karl Barth, a Swiss theologian, commented that 'the actions of the Church are a continuous crucifixion of Jesus'. When I first read that statement many years ago, I must confess I considered it to be a great exaggeration. However, I have lived to see the truth of his words. He was speaking generally, of course, because there are many exceptions, but far too often God's people behave in ways that deny the very Lord they attempt to uphold.

In the first century, six churches in Asia were singled out by Jesus because they were bringing pain to His heart. As you may know, His words to them can be found in the second and third chapters of the book of Revelation. Seven churches are mentioned there but only one is free of our Lord's condemnation.

Do you ever wonder if, when we make no effort to be reconciled to those we have offended, it brings pain to the one who died for the Church? Or, when we pursue our selfish ambition in a kingdom that is based on the self-giving attitude of Christ Jesus, do we dishonour His name? We find all through the pages of the Scriptures the call to unity, for example: 'How good and pleasant it is when brothers live together in unity!' (Psa. 133:1). And when the apostle John writes about the mutual love of Christian brothers and sisters – 'By this all men will know that you are my disciples, if you love one another' (John 13:35) – it provides possibly the greatest key to effective evangelism, and yet we put all our energies and effort into our activities and programmes. How sad that Jesus who was wounded at Calvary by His enemies, is so often wounded in His house by His friends.

FURTHER STUDY

Col. 3:12–17;
1 Pet. 4:1–11

1. What should characterise the life of believers?

2. How can we ensure that God is praised in all things?

Precious Saviour, again I plead with You to send Your Spirit among us in great power to convict us of the wrong we do You and the pain we cause You. Let your life, light and love be released in our lives and Your Church. Amen.

Glorying in the crucified

FOR READING & MEDITATION – GALATIANS 6:7–18

'God forbid that I should glory, save in the cross of our Lord Jesus Christ' (v14, AV)

Today we bring to a conclusion our meditations, in which we have reconsidered the wondrous cross. There is no spot in the universe greater than the place where Jesus gave His life for us. When I first became a Christian I just could not stop thinking about the cross – and continued to do so. Like the apostle Paul in the text before us today, I glory in it because it was there that my redemption was paid and my soul found eternal salvation.

Many men and women of this generation, especially here in the West, seem, as I said earlier, drawn to wearing a cross as a piece of jewellery. If you were to ask them why they do it, their reply would be, 'Because it's fashionable.' Some might even see the cross as representing the death of a good man and have a sympathetic interest in that idea, but few would have any concept of Him being the God-man. They would be at a loss to understand why Christians glory in it.

I have always loved the words of Sir John Bowring who, when sailing in the South China seas, saw a cross on a hill and wrote these inspiring words:

In the cross of Christ I glory,
Towering o'er the wrecks of time:
All the light of sacred story
Gathers round its head sublime.

Although the apostle Paul was converted through a vision of the glorified Christ, he did not glory in the glorified. He gloried in the crucified. That is where our glorying must be too.

FURTHER STUDY

1 Pet. 1:17–25;
Heb. 13:20–21

1. What are the truths Peter is reminding his readers of?
2. What aspects of the cross can you see in the Hebrews benediction?

Father, may I, like the apostle Paul, for ever glory in the cross of Your Son, my Saviour. May the wonder of what He did for me on that cross never diminish in my soul. This I ask in and through His peerless and precious name. Amen.

Order form

4 Easy Ways To Order

1. Phone in your credit card order: **01252 784700** (Mon–Fri, 9.30am – 4.30pm)
2. Visit our online store at **cwr.org.uk/shop**
3. Send this form together with your payment to: **CWR, Waverley Abbey House, Waverley Lane, Farnham, Surrey GU9 8EP**
4. Visit a Christian bookshop

For a list of our National Distributors, who supply countries outside the UK, visit cwr.org.uk/distributors

Your Details (required for orders and donations)

Full Name: _____ CWR ID No. (if known): _____

Home Address: _____

Postcode: _____

Telephone No. (for queries): _____ Email: _____

Publications

TITLE	QTY	PRICE	TOTAL
Total Publications			

UK P&P: up to £24.99 = **£2.99**; £25.00 and over = **FREE**

Elsewhere P&P: up to £10 = **£4.95**; £10.01 – £50 = **£6.95**; £50.01 – £99.99 = **£10**; £100 and over = **£30**

Total Publications and P&P (please allow 14 days for delivery) **A** [____]

Subscriptions* (non direct debit)

	QTY	PRICE (including P&P)			TOTAL
		UK	Europe	Elsewhere	
Every Day with Jesus (1yr, 6 issues)		£16.95	£20.95	Please contact nearest National Distributor or CWR direct	
Large Print *Every Day with Jesus* (1yr, 6 issues)		£16.95	£20.95		
Inspiring Women Every Day (1yr, 6 issues)		£16.95	£20.95		
Life Every Day (Jeff Lucas) (1yr, 6 issues)		£16.95	£20.95		
Mettle: 15–18s (1yr, 3 issues)		£14.75	£17.60		
YP's: 11–14s (1yr, 6 issues)		£16.95	£20.95		
Topz: 7–11s (1yr, 6 issues)		£16.95	£20.95		
Total Subscriptions (subscription prices already include postage and packing)				**B**	[____]

*Only use this section for subscriptions paid for by credit/debit card or cheque. For Direct Debit subscriptions see overleaf.

All CWR adult Bible reading notes are also available in **eBook** and **email subscription** format. Visit **cwr.org.uk** for further information.

Please circle which issue you would like your subscription to commence from:

JAN/FEB MAR/APR MAY/JUN JUL/AUG SEP/OCT NOV/DEC *Mettle* **JAN–APR MAY–AUG SEP–DEC**

💬 How would you like to hear from us?

We would love to keep you up to date on all aspects of the CWR ministry, including; new publications, events & courses as well as how you can support us.

If you **DO** want to hear from us on email, please tick here [ ]

If you **DO NOT** want us to contact you by post, please tick here [ ] **Continued overleaf >>**

You can update your preferences at any time by contacting our customer services team on 01252 784 700.

You can view our privacy policy online at cwr.org.uk

Payment Details

☐ I enclose a cheque/PO made payable to CWR for the amount of: **£** _____

☐ Please charge my credit/debit card.

Cardholder's Name (in BLOCK CAPITALS) _____

Card No. ☐☐☐☐ ☐☐☐☐ ☐☐☐☐ ☐☐☐☐

Expires End ☐☐ ☐☐ Security Code ☐☐☐

Gift to CWR ☐ Please send me an acknowledgement of my gift **C** [_____]

Gift Aid (your home address required, see overleaf)

giftaid it I am a UK taxpayer and want CWR to reclaim the tax on all my donations for the four years prior to this year **and on** all donations I make from the date of this Gift Aid declaration until further notice.*

Taxpayer's Full Name (in BLOCK CAPITALS) _____

Signature _____ **Date** _____

*I am a UK taxpayer and understand that if I pay less Income Tax and/or Capital Gains Tax than the amount of Gift Aid claimed on all my donations in that tax year it is my responsibility to pay any difference.

GRAND TOTAL (Total of A, B & C) [_____]

Subscriptions by Direct Debit (UK bank account holders only)

One-year subscriptions cost £16.95 (except *Mettle*: £14.75) and include UK delivery. Please tick relevant boxes and fill in the form below.

☐ *Every Day with Jesus* (1yr, 6 issues)
☐ *Large Print Every Day with Jesus* (1yr, 6 issues)
☐ *Inspiring Women Every Day* (1yr, 6 issues)
☐ *Life Every Day* (Jeff Lucas) (1yr, 6 issues)

☐ *Mettle*: 15–18s (1yr, 3 issues)
☐ *YP's*: 11–14s (1yr, 6 issues)
☐ *Topz*: 7–11s (1yr, 6 issues)

Issue to commence from

☐ Jan/Feb ☐ Jul/Aug   *Mettle* ☐ Jan–Apr
☐ Mar/Apr ☐ Sep/Oct ☐ May–Aug
☐ May/Jun ☐ Nov/Dec ☐ Sep–Dec

CWR Instruction to your Bank or Building Society to pay by Direct Debit

DIRECT Debit

Please fill in the form and send to: CWR, Waverley Abbey House, Waverley Lane, Farnham, Surrey GU9 8EP

Name and full postal address of your Bank or Building Society

To: The Manager _____ **Bank/Building Society**

Address _____

_____ Postcode _____

Name(s) of Account Holder(s)

[_____]

Branch Sort Code

☐☐ ☐☐ ☐☐

Bank/Building Society Account Number

☐☐☐☐☐☐☐☐

Originator's Identification Number

4	2	0	4	8	7

Reference

☐☐☐☐☐☐☐☐☐☐☐☐☐☐☐☐☐☐

Instruction to your Bank or Building Society

Please pay CWR Direct Debits from the account detailed in this Instruc subject to the safeguards assured by the Direct Debit Guarantee. I understand that this Instruction may remain with CWR and, if so, deta will be passed electronically to my Bank/Building Society.

Signature(s)

_____

Date

_____

Banks and Building Societies may not accept Direct Debit Instructions for some types of account